Walking in the Spirit:
A 90-Day Journey to a Spirit-Led Life

Steve Ranni

Dove Christian
Publishers

Walking in the Spirit
Published by Dove Christian Publishers
PO Box 611, Bladensburg, MD 20710 USA
https://dovechristianpublishers.com

Dove Christian
Publishers

ISBN: 978-1-957497-83-9 (Paperback)
ISBN: 978-1-957497-90-7 (Hardcover)

Library of Congress Control Number: 2026937966

Published in the United States of America

WHAT OTHERS ARE SAYING

"The best music is a result of many hours of practice in solitude. Likewise, the deepest devotionals are a glimpse into the private closet of a life walked with God. I have witnessed my brother and co-labourer in Christ, Steve Ranni, walk with God for more than 23 years. Upon these pages you read are the intimate moments between a man, husband, father, preacher and his God. May they stir you and I as they have the author into a deepening walk with Jesus."
—*Reverend Gregory Sparkes, Canadian Forces Chaplain*

"These devotionals are not only timely truths from God's Word, but are also pastoral in heart. The insights in these pages have been collected from messages shared over the course of Steve's years in pastoral ministry. His words carry a heart to see all Christians keep in step with the Spirit and know the joy that it is to call Him friend. As his son, friend, and co-labourer in the gospel, it is my privilege to endorse this work."
—*Pastor Ryan Ranni, Young Adults Pastor, Hope City Church, Fredericton New Brunswick*

"Reverend Steve Ranni brings Scripture to life through these practical and encouraging devotionals, thoughtfully drawn from years of pastoral teaching. With clarity and compassion, he guides readers into God's Word, helping them apply biblical truth to everyday life. These devotionals will strengthen your prayer life, deepen your faith, and encourage you to stand firmly on the promises of God as you grow in your walk with Him."
—*Tammy Leigh Robinson, Best-Selling Author of the NAMELESS Trilogy and Stories of Good Grief*

"Every Christian needs tools and truths to navigate life faithfully in a difficult world. We must know who God is, what He calls us to do, and who He calls us to be. Walking in the Spirit is a 90-day devotional designed to help believers do just that, as author Steve Ranni draws from decades of life and ministry experience to equip the saints in a clear and practical way. New Christians will find the tools and truths needed for the early stages of their walk, while mature believers will find their spiritual tools sharpened again. Whether you are just beginning your walk with the Spirit or have been walking with Him for many years, this devotional will equip you well for the journey.
—*Pastor Corey Betts*
Christ Community Church, Fredericton New Brunswick

This devotional is dedicated to my wife Denise, whose love, patience, and faithful support carried me through the writing of this project.

To my family, I offer this work with the prayer that these devotionals will continue to strengthen your faith and encourage your walk with the Lord for generations to come.

Above all, this work is dedicated to God. May He use it to strengthen the faith of believers, draw unbelievers to Himself, and bring glory to His name.

Foreword

Genuine spirituality is found in a life yielded to the Holy Spirit and lived in fellowship with the Lord Jesus Christ. It is the product of faith alone in the One who died for all people. Such spirituality is nurtured by a daily devotional life in which the Word of God is the "meat and drink" for one's soul.

In the following pages Pastor Steve Ranni graciously guides his readers to a personal walk through selected Bible passages in a manner that will warm the Christian's heart. The need for spiritual freshness is an ongoing reality that can only be met by Scripture. These meditations will encourage us to focus our attention on God's Word and to draw closer to the Lord.

It will become evident that these devotionals are not just sentimental thoughts. They are reflections of the author's years of Bible study, spiritual exercise and pastoral ministry. They are the words of a pastor's heart. May the Lord use them to encourage you today.

Relax, and prayerfully embrace God's truth and loving kindness.

David Doherty Th. D.,
Campus Pastor, Academic Dean, Faculty
New Brunswick Bible Institute, Victoria Corner, New Brunswick
Author of *Whosoever Will May Come, Did Jesus Die for You?*

CONTENTS

What Others Are Saying iii

Foreword vii

Introduction:
Who Is the Holy Spirit? xvii

Day 1. Walking in the Spirit 1

Day 2. A Prayer for Wisdom and Power 4

Day 3. Achieving Faith Like a Child 7

Day 4. Guard Your Heart 10

Day 5. The Hope Within Us 13

Day 6. Helper, Fan, or Follower:
The Call to True Discipleship 16

Day 7. Our Faith vs. Our Feelings 19

Day 8. The Tale of Two Wives 22

Day 9. From Triumph to Tragedy 25

Day 10. Your Most Precious Possession 28

Day 11. Ending the Worship War 31

Day 12. The Joy of the Lord 34

Day 13. Redeeming Value 37

Day 14. Are You Running For God or From God? 40

Day 15. A Lesson From the Ants 43

Day 16. Focussing on Heaven 46

Day 17. From Slavery to Sonship 49

Day 18. No Hope, False Hope, True Hope 52

Day 19. The What, Why, and How of Worship 55

Day 20. Is Sunday Still A Holy Day? 58

Day 21. From Awe to Amazing 61

Day 22. Blessings Come by Faith 64

Day 23. It's Time to Wake Up, Get Dressed, and Go to Work 67

Day 24. Controlling Our Anger ... 70

Day 25. Are You Spiritually Alive? ... 73

Day 26. Overcoming Opposition ... 76

Day 27. Five Characteristics of a Pure Heart ... 79

Day 28. The Importance of Baptism ... 82

Day 29. God's Perfect Plan ... 85

Day 30. If We Love Him… ... 88

Day 31. One Step at a Time ... 91

Day 32. Life is a Dash ... 94

Day 33. The Redeemer and the Redeemed ... 97

Day 34. Called to Serve ... 100

Day 35. In the Master's Hands ... 103

Day 36. A Call to Worship ... 106

Day 37. The Power of Encouragement (Part One) ... 109

Day 38. The Power of Encouragement (Part Two) ... 112

Day 39. Our Choices Make Us Who We Are ... 115

Day 40. Transforming Truth ... 118

Day 41. The Purpose of Praise ... 121

Day 42. Ageing With Grace ... 124

Day 43. The Importance of Handling God's Word ... 127

Day 44. Becoming Better Not Bitter ... 130

Day 45. The Power of the Promise ... 133

Day 46. Beneath the Surface ... 136

Day 47. A Lesson From a Donkey ... 139

Day 48. The Holy Spirit's Leading ... 142

Day 49. Seize the Moment and Live Life to the Fullest ... 145

Day 50. Thirsting for Christ ... 148

Day 51. The Greatest of These is Love ... 151

Day 52. Being Fully Committed ... 154

Day 53. Ending Christian Intolerance 157

Day 54. God's Promise for Protection 160

Day 55. God's Promise for Peace 163

Day 56. God's Promise of His Presence 166

Day 57. God Keep Our Land 169

Day 58. Finishing the Race with the Flame Still Burning 172

Day 59. Making A Difference 175

Day 60. Pressing On
(A Tribute to Pastor John McLean) 178

Day 61. Fighting the Good Fight 181

Day 62. Trusting the Word of God 184

Day 63. Empty Tomb or Empty Faith 187

Day 64. Staying Connected to the Vine 190

Day 65. The Lost Art of Commitment
(Calling All Men) 193

Day 66. Proclaiming Freedom 196

Day 67. Planting the Seed of Faith 199

Day 68. Experiencing Unspeakable Joy 202

Day 69. Salt and Light 205

Day 70. The Power of Prayer 208

Day 71. Standing on the Promises of God 211

Day 72. Real Love 214

Day 73. Are You Being a True Neighbour? 217

Day 74. Finding Courage in Christ 220

Day 75. A Future With Hope 223

Day 76. The Secret to Servanthood 226

Day 77. Why Do We Follow God? 229

Day 78. The Gift of Peace 232

Day 79. Demonstrating Our Faith in Difficult Times 235

Day 80. Things that Can Bring Revival 238

Day 81. Pioneers Wanted 241

Day 82. Sufficient and Sustaining Grace 244

Day 83. Handling Christian Conflict 247

Day 84. The Light Has Come 250

Day 85. The Importance of Attending Church 253

Day 86. Jesus is a Friend to the Fallen 256

Day 87. Being Equipped by God 259

Day 88. Four Verbs To Overcome Trials 262

Day 89. Get Into The Game 265

Day 90. Leaving a Godly Legacy 268

Author's Note 273

Reflection & Discussion Questions 275

Acknowledgments 277

Scripture Readings

Day 1. Galatians 5:16-25	1
Day 2. Ephesians 1:15-20	4
Day 3. Matthew 18:1-5	7
Day 4. Proverbs 4:20-27	10
Day 5. Mark 13:24-37	13
Day 6. Mark 8:34-38	16
Day 7. 2 Corinthians 5:1-10	19
Day 8. Galatians 4:21-31	22
Day 9. Matthew 21:1-11	25
Day 10. Mark 8:27-38	28
Day 11. John 4:19-24	31
Day 12. Isaiah 12:1-6	34
Day 13. Galatians 3:10-14	37
Day 14. Jonah 1:1-17	40
Day 15. Proverbs 6:6-9	43
Day 16. John 14:1-11	46
Day 17. Galatians 4:1-7	49
Day 18. Titus 2:11-15	52
Day 19. Psalm 95:1-7	55
Day 20. Exodus 20:8-11	58
Day 21. Psalm 19-1-6	61
Day 22. Galatians 3:1-9	64
Day 23. Romans 13:11-14	67
Day 24. Ephesians 4:26-31	70
Day 25. Colossians 2:13-15	73
Day 26. Nehemiah 4:1-8	76
Day 27. 2 Timothy 2:22-26	79

Day 28. Romans 6:1-11 82

Day 29. Jeremiah 29:10-14 85

Day 30. Jn 21:15-17; Pr 22:6; Mk 10:13-16 88

Day 31. Matthew 14:22-33 91

Day 32. Job 7:7-9, 9:25-26, 14:1-2 94

Day 33. Ephesians 1:7-12 97

Day 34. Galatians 5:13-14 100

Day 35. Matthew 14:15-22 103

Day 36. Romans 12:1-8 106

Day 37. Hebrews 10:24-25 109

Day 38. Hebrews 11:22-25 112

Day 39. Galatians 5:16-26 115

Day 40. Ephesians 4:11-21 118

Day 41. Psalm 150:1-6 121

Day 42. Ecclesiastes 12:1-8 124

Day 43. 2 Timothy 2:15-18 127

Day 44. Acts 27 130

Day 45. Acts 1:1-2:38 133

Day 46. Jonah 1:1-12 136

Day 47. Mark 11:1-11 139

Day 48. John 16:6-15 142

Day 49. Philippians 3:7-16 145

Day 50. John 19:16-30 148

Day 51. Galatians 5:16-23 151

Day 52. Acts 2:32-41 154

Day 53. Romans 14:1-13 157

Day 54. Isaiah 41:1-20 160

Day 55. John 14:15-27 163

Day 56. Exodus 33:12-23 166

Day 57. Revelation 4:1-11 169

Day 58. Philippians 3:12-16 172

Day 59. Ecclesiastes 9:1-10 175

Day 60. Hebrews 12:1-4 178

Day 61. Ephesians 6:11-18 181

Day 62. 2 Timothy 4:1-14 184

Day 63. 1 Corinthians 15:50-58 187

Day 64. John 15:1-13 190

Day 65. Joshua 24:11-15 193

Day 66. Isaiah 61:1-7 196

Day 67. Exodus 2:1-9 199

Day 68. 1 Peter 1:3-9 202

Day 69. Matthew 5:13-16 205

Day 70. James 5:13-16 208

Day 71. Galatians 3:15-29 211

Day 72. 1 John 4:20-5:5 214

Day 73. Luke 10:25-37 217

Day 74. Exodus 3:4-4:17 220

Day 75. Jeremiah 29:4-14 223

Day 76. Luke 17:7-10 226

Day 77. Matthew 5:1-2, 7:28-8:1 229

Day 78. Luke 2:8-14 232

Day 79. Acts 10 235

Day 80. 1 Samuel 7:1-9 238

Day 81. Philippians 1:12-26 241

Day 82. 2 Corinthians 12:6-10 244

Day 83. Galatians 2:11-14 247

Day 84. Luke 2:1-14 250

Day 85. Hebrews 10:19-25 253

Day 86. John 21:1-19 256

Day 87. Exodus 4:10-12 259

Day 88. James 1:1-12 262

Day 89. Acts 6:1-7 265

Day 90. Deuteronomy 11:18-20 268

Introduction:
Who Is the Holy Spirit?

Before we can walk in the Spirit, we must first understand who the Holy Spirit is. In the Christian faith, the Holy Spirit is not an impersonal force, influence, or some sort of feeling. He is the third Person of the Trinity—fully God, equal with the Father and the Son, and eternally existent.

Jesus affirmed this truth when He promised His disciples that after His departure, the Father would send a Helper: *"And I will ask the Father, and he will give you another Advocate, who will never leave you"* (John 14:16 NLT).

The word *'another'* here means *"one of the same kind."* Just as Jesus walked with the disciples in person, the Holy Spirit would now dwell within them.

Scripture clearly presents the Holy Spirit as a person with intellect and emotions. He speaks (Acts 13:2 NIV), teaches (John 14:26 NLT), guides (Romans 8:14 NIV), grieves (Ephesians 4:30 NIV), and intercedes for all believers (Romans 8:26–27 NKJV). These are not the actions of an impersonal force but of a divine Person who desires relationship.

Jesus referred to the Spirit using personal pronouns, saying, *"When He, the Spirit of truth, has come, He will guide you into all truth"* (John 16:13 NKJV).

The Holy Spirit possesses all the attributes of deity. He is eternal (Hebrews 9:14), all-knowing (1 Corinthians 2:10–11), all-powerful (Luke 1:35), and present everywhere (Psalm 139:7–10). In Acts 5:3–4,

Peter equates lying to the Holy Spirit with lying to God, clearly identifying Him as divine.

From creation onward, the Spirit has been actively at work: Scripture says that *"The Spirit of God was hovering over the surface of the waters"* (Genesis 1:2 NLT). The same Spirit who participated in creation now lives within every believer.

The Holy Spirit is holy—set apart and pure in all His ways. He does not lead believers into sin but into righteousness and truth. His character is revealed through the fruit He produces in the lives of those who walk with Him: *"But the fruit of the Spirit is love, joy, peace, patience, kindness, goodness, faithfulness, gentleness, and self-control"* (Galatians 5:22–23 NLT). These qualities reflect the very nature of God. As we walk in step with the Spirit, His character becomes increasingly evident in our lives.

The Holy Spirit plays a vital role in the life of every Christian. He convicts the world of sin, righteousness, and judgment (John 16:8, NIV). He regenerates the believer at salvation (Titus 3:5 NLT). He indwells every follower of Christ (Romans 8:11 NKJV), sealing them as God's own (Ephesians 1:13–14 NIV).

The Spirit also empowers believers to live the Christian life: *"For the Spirit God gave us does not make us timid, but gives us power, love and self-discipline"* (2 Timothy 1:7 NIV). Walking in the Spirit is not about self-effort but a daily dependence on His strength and guidance.

A Spirit-Led life lives in ongoing fellowship with Him—listening to His voice, yielding to His leading, and relying on His power. Paul exhorts believers, *"So I say, let the Holy Spirit guide your lives. Then you won't be doing what your sinful nature craves"* (Galatians 5:16 NLT).

This 90-day journey is an invitation for you to know the Holy Spirit more deeply—not merely as a doctrine to understand, but as a divine Companion to walk with and to be led by. He is God's abiding presence within us, leading us into truth, and empowering us to live lives that honour the Father.

As you embark on this journey, may you come to know the Holy Spirit not just as the third Person of the Trinity, but as your Helper, Guide, Comforter, and Friend.

DAY 1

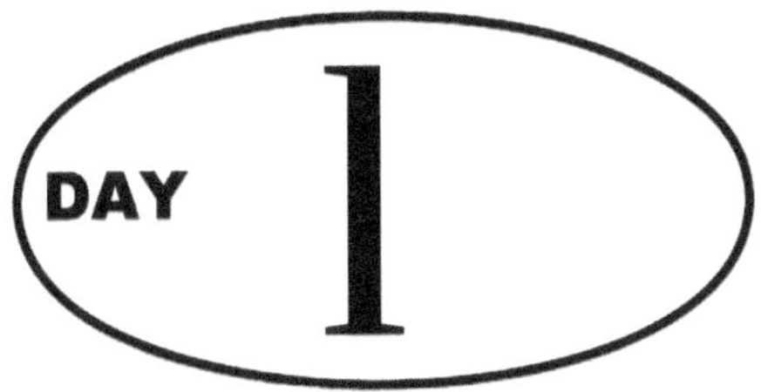

WALKING IN THE SPIRIT

Read: Galatians 5:16-25

The Christian life is not a static experience or a sprint—it's a daily walk. When the Apostle Paul wrote to the Galatians, he was addressing believers who, like we do, struggled to live out their faith in a world full of competing voices that can sometimes be extremely deafening. "*Walk by the Spirit,*" he said, "*and you will not gratify the desires of the flesh.*" (vs16 NIV) It sounds simple, yet it touches the deepest tension in every believer's heart.

When someone becomes a Christian, they are given new life. The Holy Spirit takes up residence within us, renewing our minds and hearts. Now, even though we have been made new, our old nature—the flesh—still lingers and fights for control whenever it can. These two natures, Paul says, are in constant conflict (vs. 16–18). The flesh craves comfort, pride, and self-satisfaction; the Spirit draws us toward surrender, humility, and holiness. To follow the Spirit means acknowledging this battle—not denying it, not excusing it—but learning to yield our will to God's daily leading.

How you live your life points to who you live it for. Every decision, every word, and every attitude reveals the source of your strength. Paul contrasts the *"acts of the flesh"* (vs. 19–21) with the *"fruit of the Spirit"* (vs. 22–23). The works of the flesh are things we produce on our own—selfishness, anger, impurity, envy. The fruit of the Spirit, however, is what God produces in us as we abide in Him—love, joy, peace, patience, kindness, goodness, faithfulness, gentleness, and self-control.

Notice the difference between *"acts"* and *"fruit."* Acts are what *we* do; fruit is what *God* grows. Our part is not to strive harder but to stay rooted in the Spirit's presence. When our roots go deep into God's Word and we mature in Christ, His fruit becomes visible in our lives.

The gospel itself is reflected here. The struggle between the flesh and Spirit points us back to the cross—where Jesus carried the full weight of our sin so we would not have to. If we ignore or downplay our sin, we will minimize the power of His sacrifice. The more we understand what He saved us from, the more deeply we will appreciate His grace.

Paul connects this truth beautifully in (Philippians 2:12–13 NIV): *"Continue to work out your salvation with fear and trembling, for it is God who works in you to will and to act in order to fulfill His good purpose."* We do not *"work for"* salvation—Christ already accomplished that completely. But we *work it out* by cooperating with the Spirit's transforming power. Spiritual growth requires participation. Every day we must choose to walk where He leads, to obey when it's difficult, and to trust when things seem unclear.

An unknown author once said, *"Sin and the child of God may occasionally meet, but they cannot permanently sit together."* This is the reality of life in the Spirit. There will be moments when we stumble—when the flesh momentarily wins. But if the Spirit truly dwells within us, we will not stay comfortable there because He will convict, correct, and eventually call us back to fellowship. Walking in the Spirit means we keep moving forward and getting back up when we fall.

Walking implies progress and direction. It's not running ahead of God or standing still in complacency—it's step-by-step obedience. It's daily choices like forgiving when it's hard, showing kindness when it's inconvenient, or choosing peace over resentment. These are the quiet steps that form a Spirit-led life.

The truth is, walking in the Spirit doesn't happen by accident. It requires intentionality. It's taking a pause before you speak, praying before you act, and listening before you decide. The more we walk with Him, the more we learn His rhythm and recognize His voice.

So, as you embark on this devotional journey, ask yourself: Whose voice am I following? Am I reacting from my flesh, or responding in the Spirit?

The Spirit's path may not always be easy, but it leads to freedom, not bondage; peace, not chaos; life, not death. May the timeless truths of this 90-day devotional help you keep in step with Him—one day at a time. If you are open to the Spirit's leading, you will find that His fruit will quietly take root in your heart, transforming you from the inside out.

"Holy Spirit, I want to walk closely with You. Please teach me through these devotionals to recognize Your voice above all others. Help me to crucify the desires of the flesh and to yield fully to Your leading. Produce Your fruit in me so that my life points others to Jesus, Amen."

DAY 2

A Prayer for Wisdom and Power

Read: Ephesians 1:15-20

Prayer is one of the greatest gifts God has given us. It isn't just a religious duty—it's a real conversation with the God who loves us. As you continue to walk through this devotional, my prayer is that you will be strengthened in your faith and encouraged by the Holy Spirit. Prayer truly changes things. It shapes our hearts, guides our choices, and brings us closer to the One who knows us best.

In Ephesians 1:15–20, the apostle Paul prays three powerful prayers for the believers in Ephesus. These same prayers can help guide and strengthen our spiritual journey today.

Paul begins by praying that God would give believers spiritual wisdom so they can know Him better. (Ephesians 1:17 NLT) says, "Asking God, the glorious Father of our Lord Jesus Christ, to give you spiritual wisdom and insight so that you might grow in your knowledge of God."

This kind of wisdom doesn't come from experience alone. It comes from God Himself as we read His Word, pray, and seek His guidance. When we ask God for wisdom, He is faithful to give it. (Proverbs 2:6 NLT) reminds us, "For the Lord grants wisdom! From his mouth come knowledge and understanding." As you continue this devotional journey, ask God daily for wisdom—for your life, your family, your decisions, and your spiritual growth. He will guide you.

Next, Paul prays that believers will fully grasp the hope they have in Christ. Paul wrote, "I pray that your hearts will be flooded with light so that you can understand the confident hope he has given to those he called—his holy people who are his rich and glorious inheritance." (Ephesians 1:18 NLT) This verse tells us something incredible: God calls His people His inheritance. That means He treasures you. You belong to Him. This hope is not fragile or uncertain. It is strong, steady, and unchanging because it's rooted in the finished work of Jesus Christ.

When we understand who we are in Christ, His light pushes back the darkness that tries to pull us down. John declares that, *"The light shines in the darkness, and the darkness can never extinguish it."* (John 1:5 NLT) We are God's people, bought with the precious blood of Jesus. This truth gives us purpose, confidence, and hope as we walk with Christ. As Paul prayed for the Ephesian believers, we too can pray that God's light floods our hearts and helps us live each day with a clear sense of hope and identity in Him.

Paul ends his prayer by asking God to help believers understand the greatness of His power. (Ephesians 1:19–20 NLT) says, *"I also pray that you will understand the incredible greatness of God's power for us who believe him. This is the same mighty power that raised Christ from the dead and seated him in the place of honour at God's right hand in the heavenly realms."* The same power that raised Jesus from the dead is at work in the life of every believer. This power gives us strength when we feel weak, courage when we feel afraid, and hope when circumstances seem overwhelming.

Paul understood this deeply when he said, *"This is a trustworthy saying, and everyone should accept it: 'Christ Jesus came into the world to save sinners'—and I am the worst of them all."* (1 Timothy 1:15 NLT) And in (Ephesians 3:12 NLT) he said, *"Because of Christ and our faith in him, we can now come boldly and confidently into God's presence."* This resurrection power is not distant or unreachable. Through prayer, faith, and the Holy Spirit, God equips and empowers every believer to live out their calling.

Paul's prayer in Ephesians 1 is a prayer we can make our own today. As you continue on this devotional journey, may God's Word take root in your heart. May His wisdom guide you, His hope strengthen you, and His power sustain you. Remember, God is faithful, and He will walk with you through every season ahead.

> *"Heavenly Father, thank You for Your love, Your grace, and the gift of prayer. I ask today for Your wisdom—help me grow in my understanding of who You are. Flood my heart with Your light so I can fully grasp the hope I have in Christ. Help me understand and experience the power You make available to all who believe. Strengthen my faith, guide my steps, and draw me closer to You every day. In Jesus name I pray, Amen."*

ACHIEVING FAITH LIKE A CHILD

Read: Matthew 18:1-5

Our text for today comes from Matthew 18:1-5, where the disciples ask Jesus a question. They inquired about who would be the greatest in the kingdom of heaven. However, Jesus responded by demonstrating that they were asking the wrong question. Their question is similar to asking, "How can I be a 5-star Christian?" or "What does it mean to be truly spiritual in God's eyes?" These are the wrong questions because true spirituality is found in being converted or saved. The Greek word for *"converted"* means *"changed or turned."*

Childlike faith is not about being *"truly spiritual."* Instead, it revolves around a turning point in our lives where we accept Christ and His message with honesty and loyalty, like a child, relying on Him wholeheartedly.

Childlike faith is about having a different perspective, one focused on eternal rather than temporary rewards. It's easy to lose our eternal perspective and become distracted by earthly pursuits, even within the Church. We tend to compete for promotions or status, sometimes at the expense of the heavenly treasures that await us.

Do you remember the carefree days of childhood when you didn't worry about responsibilities and obligations? Life was simpler, and stress didn't overwhelm you. Although responsibilities have their place, childlike faith encourages us to embrace God's perspective and look beyond temporary pleasures.

To have a childlike faith, we must cultivate three attitudes:

1. Humility

Children have a remarkable capacity for humility. They don't see differences in race, background, or gender as a means to elevate or diminish others. They perceive the world with simplicity and without stress. As Christians, we should also strive to maintain this childlike humility. In Matthew 18:4, Jesus said, *"Whoever humbles himself as this little child is the greatest in the kingdom of heaven."*

2. Teachability

Children display a remarkable eagerness to learn and a desire for knowledge. As we grow older, we may tend to think we should have all the answers. While the Bible offers many answers, faith means putting trust in God based on spiritual understanding, not irrefutable proof. We don't need to know everything, but we believe in the One who does.

3. Dependence

Children are dependent on others and often ask for help without hesitation. In the same way, Christians must remain utterly dependent on God. 2 Corinthians 1:9-10 emphasizes our need to rely on Him, especially in times of trouble. God is not looking for "5-star Christians." However, He is looking for dependent followers who trust in His strength.

Dependence on God is crucial, as it reminds us that we can't handle life's challenges on our own. When we ask God for help, He can change our lives in significant ways.

Childlike faith is marked by humility, teachability, and dependence. If you're not a Christian, I encourage you to accept Christ into your life. Conversion takes place when someone acknowledges that they have sinned and have fallen short of God's standards. They humble themselves before their Creator and ask for forgiveness, and by the Holy Spirit's conviction, they understand that they cannot navigate this life alone and that they need a Saviour to change and inspire them.

For Christians, this devotion should serve as a reminder to return to the humility, teachability, and dependence of childlike faith. By humbling ourselves and relying on God, we can experience the joy and grace that come from walking with Him. We don't need to have all the answers; we need to have faith. Remember, God is looking for dependent followers who trust in His strength.

Having a childlike faith is essential to having a lasting faith. The basis of our faith is that we need a Saviour who will rescue us and renew us from the inside out! We need a Saviour who will lead us and give us strength and guidance for every single day and every single situation that we encounter! If you humble yourself before God, and allow yourself to be taught by Him, and constantly depend on Him, He will renew and refresh you in love and in grace, forever and ever. Amen!

> "Oh Lord, how I long for a childlike faith. A faith that is surrendered to You and one where I fully trust in You and Your promises. I humble myself before You today. My desire is to be teachable and dependent upon You so that I can become more like You. Amen."

DAY 4

GUARD YOUR HEART

Read: Proverbs 4:20-27

John Flavel wisely observed, "The greatest difficulty in conversion is to win the heart to God, and the greatest difficulty after conversion is to keep the heart with God." Few statements capture the Christian life more clearly. Scripture consistently points us to the heart because the heart represents the center of who we are—our desires, choices, and direction. When the Bible commands us to "guard your heart," it invites us into a lifelong practice of spiritual attentiveness. In this devotional, we will consider the reconstruction and the regulation of the heart, as well as several practical ways to live out this biblical instruction.

The Reconstruction of the Heart

Christianity is, at its core, a transforming work of God in the heart. Just as physical life depends on the health of the physical heart, spiritual life depends on the condition of the inner person. James Stowell describes the heart as the *"comprehensive term for the authentic person"*—

the place where motives are formed and decisions are made, and where God looks most closely.

Scripture makes it clear that God must first give us a new heart. In (Ezekiel 36:26–27 NLT), God promises, *"I will give you a new heart, and I will put a new spirit in you. I will take out your stony, stubborn heart and give you a tender, responsive heart."* Because of sin, every human heart is corrupted from within. Like a worm hidden inside an apple, sin works internally before its effects are ever seen outwardly in words or actions (see Jeremiah 17:9 NLT).

While human efforts—education, counselling, or self-improvement—can modify behaviour, only God can truly change the heart. Redemption and cleansing come through Christ alone (Hebrews 9:14 NLT). As the hymn reminds us, nothing but the blood of Jesus can make us whole.

The Regulation of the Heart

Once the heart is made new, it must also be guarded. (Proverbs 4:23 NLT) urges us, *"Guard your heart above all else, for it determines the course of your life."* To guard means to watch carefully, to protect diligently, and to supply what nourishes growth—chiefly, the Word of God.

Jesus taught that what fills the heart will eventually shape our lives. *"What you say flows from what is in your heart"* (Luke 6:45 NLT). A heart shaped by God produces godly fruit. This is why Christianity is never merely external; a right heart leads to a righteous life.

God also calls for wholehearted devotion. *"O my son, give me your heart. May your eyes take delight in following my ways"* (Proverbs 23:26 NLT). True worship begins where no one else sees—in the heart. Without a guarded heart, spiritual habits become empty routines.

Practical Steps to Guard Your Heart

Keep Your Heart Full

Fill your heart with Christ, the cross, and eternal truth (Colossians 3:1–3 NLT). A heart full of God leaves little room for sin.

Keep Your Heart Pure

Focus your thoughts on what honours the Lord (Philippians 4:8 NLT), and actively resist pride, lust, and greed (1 Peter

1:15–16 NLT).

Keep Your Heart Loyal
Give your heart fully to Christ, serving Him alone (Matthew 22:37 NLT).

Watch What You Say
Let your words build others up, not tear them down (Proverbs 18:21 NLT; Ephesians 4:29 NLT).

Watch What You Watch
Be mindful of what you allow into your mind (Psalm 101:3 NLT; Matthew 6:22–23 NLT).

Watch Where You Walk
Choose godly companions who strengthen your faith (Proverbs 13:20 NLT; 1 Corinthians 15:33, NLT).

In conclusion, guarding your heart involves prayer, resisting temptation, immersing yourself in God's Word, exercising faith, and maintaining communion with Christ. When these biblical guidelines are implemented, Philippians 4:7 assures us that, *"The peace of God, which surpasses all understanding, will guard your hearts and minds through Christ Jesus."* So, if you diligently guard your heart, your life will be rooted in God's peace and righteousness.

"Jesus, I desire a pure heart. May the lyrics of Purify My Heart by Brian Doerksen resound today, "Refiner's fire, my heart's one desire is to be holy, set apart for You, Lord. I choose to be holy, set apart for You, my Master, Ready to do Your will." Amen."

The Hope Within Us

Read: Mark 13:24-37

How often do we find ourselves caught in the tension of a promise unfulfilled? In a world where broken promises are almost expected, we, too, at times stumble in keeping our word. However, as Christians, we are called to a different standard. One that is reflected in the promises of our faithful God. Today, we explore the theme of hope embedded in God's promises, drawn from Mark 13:24-37.

Mark's Gospel outlines a profound prediction of Christ's return. Verses 24-27 vividly describe cosmic events signalling the Son of Man's coming. While the exact day of the second advent is unknown, the certainty of His return remains. We are living in a *Between Time,* a space marked by both Christ's first and second coming. As author William Willomon puts it, *"We are between the now and the not yet."* Our existence in this in-between time is intentional, orchestrated by God for a divine purpose.

Mark urges us to be prepared, drawing an analogy from the fig tree. While we may not know the precise timing, we can discern the signs of the times. Living in a state of readiness involves daily routines infused with God's presence. It's not about anticipating an event but living a life consistent with our faith. When John Wesley was asked what he would do if Christ returned tomorrow, he replied, *"I would go to bed and go to sleep; wake up in the morning, and go on with my work, for I would want Him to find me doing what he had appointed."* The challenge is to live in such a way that our faith is evident, regardless of when Christ returns.

Mark 13:30-31 unveils a promise that transcends the temporal nature of this world. Heaven and earth will pass away, but God's words and promises are eternal. This promise is the foundation of our hope. Living with eternity in mind, we face trials and challenges with the assurance that our salvation is secure.

As we eagerly await Christ's return, we are commanded to *"Keep Watch"* (Mark 13:35-37). This call goes beyond mere anticipation; it's a command to be vigilant, prepared, and active in God's kingdom work. Keeping watch involves prayer, both for ourselves and for those who have yet to experience the transforming power of Christ. It requires being active in ministry and the building of God's kingdom.

Having served in the military with one six-month tour in Bosnia, I equate this to soldiers on active duty; Christians are called to live alert and ready. A soldier doesn't know when the call to action will come, but training, discipline, and vigilance shape daily life. Even in moments of rest, readiness is never abandoned. In the same way, believers are not anxiously scanning the horizon but faithfully living out their calling, equipped with the armour of God and attentive to their Commander's voice. Our hope does not make us passive; it prepares us, grounds us, and keeps us faithful until Christ returns.

The urgency to be prepared and actively prepare others stems from our role in God's plan for salvation. Living with hope compels us to share that hope with others. In the midst of a world moving closer to its final days, the church stands as the beacon of hope. We are God's chosen plan for the salvation of humanity, and there is no Plan B.

"Heavenly Father, I thank You for the hope embedded in Your promises. As I navigate this 'Between Time,' help me to be vigilant, prepared, and actively involved in Your Kingdom work. May my life reflect the certainty of Your Word, and may I share this hope with those who desperately need to hear it, Amen".

"Heavenly Father, I thank You for the hope embedded in Your promises. As I navigate this 'Between Time,' help me to be vigilant, prepared, and actively involved in Your Kingdom work. May my life reflect the certainty of Your Word, and may I share this hope with those who desperately need to hear it, Amen".

DAY 6

HELPER, FAN, OR FOLLOWER: THE CALL TO TRUE DISCIPLESHIP

Read: Mark 8:34-38

Today, I invite you to ponder the question: Am I a helper, a fan, or a true follower of Jesus Christ? In a world filled with distractions and half-hearted commitments, it's essential to examine the depth of our relationship with our Saviour.

Our devotion centres around Mark 8:34-38, where Jesus delivered a powerful message to the crowd. He gathered His disciples and called on the multitude to consider the cost of following Him. He said, *"If any of you wants to be my follower, you must give up your own way, take up your cross, and follow me."* These words hold profound significance for anyone who desires to walk in the footsteps of Christ.

It's crucial to distinguish between a true follower of Christ and a mere fan. Many in the crowd that followed Jesus during His earthly ministry were not genuine followers; they were mere spectators seeking benefits without considering the cost of discipleship. Sadly, this remains true in today's culture and even within our churches.

Jesus discouraged casual association with Him. In Luke 9:57-62, we see examples of individuals who wanted to follow Jesus but were hesitant when confronted with the sacrifices required. The truth is, He wants followers, not fans.

Fans are like spectators who enjoy the show, seeking entertainment and benefits without full commitment. They are content with a comfortable seat in the back row, not willing to make the sacrifices demanded of true followers.

To become a true follower of Christ, one must be willing to surrender, sacrifice, and serve selflessly, regardless of the benefits. We must be ready to face hardships and challenges for the sake of the Kingdom of God.

Just as Jesus doesn't want fans, He also doesn't need helpers. Helpers are those who contribute minimally when it suits them. They offer assistance but lack a full commitment to Christ's cause.

We must understand that God, the Creator of the universe, doesn't need our help. In Genesis 1:1, we learn that God created everything. He desires followers who will give their all to His purpose and calling.

To motivate us in our journey of discipleship, Jesus offers an incredible promise in (Matthew 19:28 NLT): *"I assure you that when the world is made new and the Son of Man sits upon his glorious throne, you who have been my followers will also sit on twelve thrones, judging the twelve tribes of Israel."* Verse 29 then tells us that those who have given up houses, family, and possessions for His sake will receive a hundredfold in return and inherit eternal life. The rewards of true discipleship far surpass any earthly gains.

In conclusion, we all face a choice. Are we willing to give up our own way, take up our cross, and follow Jesus? Are we ready to be true followers rather than mere fans or casual helpers? The choice we make will determine where we stand in the Kingdom of God.

Our commitment to Christ should be unwavering, regardless of the challenges and sacrifices we encounter.

As we move forward, let's rekindle our first love for Christ and fully embrace His devotion to us. Let's comprehend the depth of His love, sacrifice, and the call He extends to us. By answering His call, we can truly become devoted followers, bearing our cross and following

Him. Remember that He is calling and pursuing us, and our response will determine the depth of our relationship with Him.

> *"Lord, I want to be a follower, not just a fan or a helper. I now know that you don't desire fans and you don't need helpers. May the Holy Spirit convict me in the areas I need to change so that I will surrender, sacrifice, and selflessly serve You all the days of my life, Amen."*

OUR FAITH VS. OUR FEELINGS

Read: 2 Corinthians 5:1-10

In our journey of faith, there are times when we face challenges that make us question God's presence in our lives. Have you ever found yourself in a situation where you didn't feel God's comforting touch or hear His reassuring voice? It's a common experience, and today, we'll look at the topic of "Faith vs. Feelings."

As Christians, we are called to walk by faith, not by sight, and definitely not solely by our feelings. The challenge arises because we believe in a God we can't see, hear, or touch. I believe most Christians want to experience Him and feel His presence as often as possible. But what happens when there's nothing? When our struggles lead us to plead with God for a sign, a touch, or a healing, and all we encounter is silence?

This struggle is universal, and it often leads us to doubt whether we're truly experiencing God's presence in our lives. Today, let's explore the dynamic between our faith and our feelings.

In times of spiritual drought, it's not uncommon to encounter individuals who claim to feel God's presence everywhere. They share stories of conversations with God, miraculous interventions, and divine guidance in everyday activities. While these testimonies are often valid, we may wonder, *"Why don't I experience God in the same way?"*

The truth is, feelings can be fickle. They come and go, influenced by various factors. Consider the example of watching an emotional video or experiencing a moving performance on a talent show. While these moments can evoke intense emotions, they don't necessarily equate to feeling the presence of God.

The Bible acknowledges that not always feeling God's presence is a reality. Psalms 77 and 88 present raw, honest expressions of individuals questioning God's closeness during times of trouble. Even David, the author of Psalm 23, experienced moments of feeling abandoned by God. The Bible reminds us that we won't always feel God's presence, and that's okay.

The disciples in John 6 exemplify a common human tendency. Despite witnessing Jesus' miracles, they asked for more signs. Similarly, we might find ourselves wanting God to prove His presence through extraordinary signs. However, God doesn't always reveal Himself in the ways we expect.

Moreover, sin can create a barrier between God and us. When we allow sin to persist without repentance, it hardens our hearts and hinders our ability to feel God's presence. Just as trust is lost in a relationship when one party acts against the other, sin creates distance and prevents us from sensing God's intimate closeness.

If you find yourself distant from God, there's hope. Confession, repentance, and seeking forgiveness are powerful ways to soften a hardened heart. As (1 John 1:9 NLT) assures us, *"If we confess our sins to him, he is faithful and just to forgive us and to cleanse us from every wrong."* Just as David prayed in Psalm 51, asking God to purify and renew him, we too can turn back to God for cleansing.

In conclusion, the journey of faith involves seasons of feeling God's presence and times when His closeness seems elusive. It's essential to recognize that feelings are not the sole indicators of God's presence. Even when we don't feel Him, God remains faithful. So, if you're currently in a season of spiritual dryness, don't give up. Trust that God is with you, even when you can't feel His presence. As (Joshua 1:9 NLT) declares,

"Be strong and courageous… for the Lord your God is with you wherever you go." Let's personalize this truth in our lives, knowing that the Lord **OUR** God is with **US** wherever **WE** go.

> *"Lord, remind me today that you are with me at all times, and that my faith is not based on my feelings. If there is anything in my life that displeases You, I pray that I will repent from it. I am reminded today that You are near even when I don't sense Your presence, and that You promise to never leave me or forsake me, Amen."*

DAY 8

THE TALE OF TWO WIVES

Read: Galatians 4:21-31

In Galatians 4:21–31, the Apostle Paul invites us to look back into the book of Genesis and consider a familiar but complex family story. It's the story of Abraham, his two wives—Sarah and Hagar—and their sons, Isaac and Ishmael. Paul uses this account as an illustration, or allegory, to help believers understand a deeper spiritual truth. His goal is not to retell history for its own sake, but to show the difference between living under the law and living in the freedom of God's grace.

At first glance, the story feels distant from our modern lives. Yet the issues Paul addresses are very close to home. We all wrestle with impatience, self-effort, and the temptation to *"help God out"* when His promises seem slow in coming. In that way, Abraham's story mirrors our own.

Abraham and Sarah had received a clear promise from God: they would have a son through whom God would build a great nation. But as years passed and Sarah remained unable to conceive, they grew weary of waiting. Instead of trusting God's timing, they acted according to human reasoning. Sarah offered her servant Hagar to Abraham, and Ishmael was born through that arrangement. Later, when Sarah was well beyond childbearing years, God miraculously fulfilled His promise, and Isaac was born.

Paul explains that these two births represent two very different ways of living. Ishmael was born through human effort, while Isaac was born by God's promise. One was natural; the other was supernatural. One came from impatience; the other from faith.

Paul then draws a striking comparison. Hagar represents Mount Sinai and the law—life lived by rules, obligation, and self-effort. Sarah represents God's promise and grace—life received as a gift, not earned. The tension between Ishmael and Isaac reflects the ongoing struggle believers experience between the old sinful nature and the new life given by the Spirit.

This conflict should not surprise us. Paul reminds us elsewhere that the flesh and the Spirit are constantly opposed to one another. Even as believers, we feel this tension. We want to please God, yet we still battle old habits, wrong motives, and the desire to control outcomes ourselves. Our study today in Galatians reminds us that this struggle is part of the Christian journey, but it is not meant to define how we live.

Paul's message is clear: grace and law cannot live side by side as equals. When we try to live by grace while still clinging to legalism, we end up frustrated and burdened. The law demands performance; grace invites trust. The law produces slavery; grace produces freedom.

This leads us to three important lessons for our lives today.

First, as believers, we are children of promise. Just as Isaac was born because of God's power and faithfulness, we are made new through spiritual rebirth. Salvation is not something we achieve through effort or obedience alone—it is a gift we receive by faith. We belong to God not because of what we have done, but because of what Christ has done for us.

Second, the battle between flesh and Spirit is real. Like Ishmael mocking Isaac, our old nature resists the work of the Spirit in our lives. This does not mean we are failing as Christians; it means we are human. The key is learning to rely on the Spirit rather than returning to self-reliance or rule-keeping to feel secure.

Third, we must choose grace over legalism. Paul's words are strong: the child of slavery will not share the inheritance with the child of promise. Living under grace means letting go of the need to earn God's approval. It means resting in Christ's finished work and allowing the Spirit to shape our obedience from the inside.

Jesus Himself invites us into this freedom. He tells us that His yoke is easy and His burden is light. The Christian life was never meant to be lived under crushing pressure or constant fear of failure. It is meant to be lived in trust, humility, and joyful dependence on God.

Paul's allegory challenges us to ask an honest question: are we living like children of promise, or are we slipping back into slavery? The good news is that God continually calls us back to grace. When we stumble, He does not invite us to try harder—He invites us to trust deeper.

> "Lord, help me understand this truth not just with my mind, but with my heart. Teach me to live as a child of promise, resting in Your grace and walking by Your Spirit. Free me from self-effort and fear, and lead me into the joy and freedom You have promised, Amen."

FROM TRIUMPH TO TRAGEDY

Palm Sunday, a day etched in history when Jesus, hailed as a King, entered Jerusalem triumphantly. Excitement was in the air, and a multitude, perhaps even thousands of people, lined the streets, waving palm branches, celebrating His grand entrance. Little did they know, this event marked a pivotal turning point in Jesus' ministry. What the people didn't know was that the Messiah was about to go from triumph to tragedy.

In today's reading, we witness the triumphant entry of Jesus into Jerusalem. The crowds spread their garments on the road, cut branches from trees, and proclaimed, *"Praise God for the Son of David! Blessings on the one who comes in the name of the Lord! Praise God in the highest heaven!"* (Matthew 21:9 NLT) It was a ticker-tape parade of divine proportions, reminiscent of victory celebrations after World War II.

As believers, we may not experience such grand parades, but the principle remains: genuine believers will eventually move from the trials of this life to a triumphant entry into eternity with the Lord. While on Earth, we will endure difficulties, challenges, and tragedies, but our ultimate reward is in heaven.

The cheering and praise Jesus received on that road were well-deserved. He performed miracles, fed thousands, healed the sick, and demonstrated His divine power. Even amidst the praise, Jesus remained humble, deflecting the glory to His Heavenly Father. The Apostle Paul encourages us to *"Love each other with genuine affection, and take delight in honouring each other"* (Romans 12:10 NLT). Recognizing and honouring one another's service is vital, providing encouragement in the journey of faith.

There is a story about a missionary named Henry C. Morrison. He and his wife were missionaries in Africa for over 40 years. Returning, he wondered if anyone would meet them at the docks when their ship arrived. They didn't know that President Teddy Roosevelt was on their ship. Thousands were on the dock waving banners that read "Welcome Home." Henry thought they were there for him and his wife. Later that night, he expressed his frustration to his wife that no one was there to welcome them home. She lovingly replied, *"Henry, you have forgotten something, you're not home yet!"* As believers, our ultimate welcome is not on Earth but in heaven. The Bible assures us, *"Blessed are those who die in the Lord from now on. Yes, says the Spirit, they are blessed indeed, for they will rest from their hard work; for their good deeds follow them!"* (Revelation 14:13 NLT) Earthly recognition may falter, but our deeds and faithfulness will echo in eternity.

The elation of the crowd on Palm Sunday starkly contrasts with the tragic events that unfold later in Mark 15. The same people who once praised Him now mocked and crucified Him. Jesus went from triumph to tragedy in a short span.

Life's unpredictability mirrors this shift. Political leaders praised today might face criticism tomorrow. Expectations unmet often lead to disappointment and rejection. Even in Christian service, leaders may experience highs of praise only to be met with disdain when expectations fall short.

Jesus' teachings contradicted the people's desires for a political uprising. He emphasized servanthood, not conquest, leading to a quick shift in public opinion. He declared, *"For those who exalt themselves will be humbled, and those who humble themselves will be exalted."* (Luke 14:11 NLT) True service performed in humility will find its reward in heaven.

As we navigate life's transitions, from triumphs to tragedies, and as we serve in various capacities, let Matthew 6:1-2 guide our hearts. Jesus cautioned against practising righteousness for the sake of human recognition. Earthly praise may come and go, but our Heavenly Father sees our deeds. Our ultimate reward is not in the fleeting cheers of this world but in the eternal embrace of our Saviour.

So, as we journey together, let's hold onto the example of Jesus. His humility in the face of shifting praise teaches us to fix our gaze on eternity. In heaven, where every faithful servant will receive a lasting reward, our praise will endure. Until then, let us serve with humility, knowing that our true welcome awaits us in the arms of our Heavenly Father.

> *"Father in heaven, I only want your praise and not the fleeting praises from people on this earth. I pray that I will remain humble so that on that day when I meet you face to face, you will say to me, "Well done, my good and faithful servant." May I serve you today and in the days ahead with this attitude. In Jesus name I ask these things, Amen."*

YOUR MOST PRECIOUS POSSESSION

Read: Mark 8:27-38

Have you ever considered the most expensive, prized possessions in the world? Some people own gold-plated, diamond-studded iPhones worth millions, vintage cars that cost tens of millions, or even rare stamps worth a small fortune. My daughter bought a little stuffed toy at a thrift shop recently for one dollar. She resold it for $60 because it was deemed a collector's item. While these possessions may be cherished by their owners, if you're a Christian, you possess something far more valuable, and it's not a material thing.

According to Jesus, your most treasured possession is your soul. In the gospel of Matthew, He posed two essential questions: *«And what do you benefit if you gain the whole world but lose your own soul? Is anything worth more than your soul?"* (Matthew 16:26 NLT)

Your soul is worth more than any earthly possession, and it will endure long after the world has passed away. It will outlast the stars and the planets. It holds immeasurable value because God has placed eternity in the hearts of every person from the moment of conception.

It wasn't always eternal, as only God is eternal in both directions. However, since your conception, God has infused your soul with the potential for an eternal existence.

Let this sink in: your soul far surpasses the riches of this world. It's worth more than the biggest bank account, the most extensive stock portfolio, and the most dazzling of gems. To put it simply, the value of your soul is beyond measure.

In Mark 8:27-38, Jesus highlighted the significance of the soul and offered insights into discipleship. If we intend to be Spirit-led followers of Christ, we need to understand and treasure our souls, not just ours but also the souls of others.

In Matthew 16, Jesus asked His disciples a pivotal question, *"Who do you say I am?"* Peter, responding on behalf of the disciples, answered, *"You are the Messiah."* This moment was crucial because it moved beyond what others said about Jesus to what the disciples believed in their hearts. Your faith cannot rely on what others say but must be a personal confession of your own.

This personal confession involves declaring, *"Jesus is Lord."* Your salvation hinges on confessing with your mouth and believing in your heart. Romans 10:9-10 affirms this, emphasizing that it is with your heart that you believe and are justified, and it is with your mouth that you confess and are saved.

As believers, we publicly declare our faith through baptism. It is an act that mirrors the early Christian's declaration when they would confess, *"Jesus is Lord,"* even in the face of Roman persecution. Your public confession of faith at baptism signifies your willingness to be a true follower and disciple of Christ.

In Mark 8:33-34, when Jesus began to tell His disciples about His impending suffering and death, Peter was quick to rebuke Him. Peter's ego-driven response was focused on success, not suffering. Sometimes, we also hesitate to accept challenging news, fearing it may harm our ego or pride.

To be a true disciple of Christ, you must remove your ego from the throne of your life. You need to accept God's perspective, which often differs from the world's view. Check your ego when it leads to legalism, impure thoughts, guilt, worry, discouragement, criticism, frustration, or fear. These signs indicate that you're viewing things from a worldly perspective rather than from God's.

We all grapple with our ego at times. But when you start feeling and acting like the world, remember that a true disciple seeks to view life from God's perspective. This shift enables us to treasure not only our souls but also the souls of others, promoting a deep desire to reach the lost with the love of Christ.

Being a disciple of Christ goes beyond mere belief—it's a lifelong commitment to follow, learn, and serve. As you continue to follow Christ, embrace the preciousness of your soul and the souls of others. Understand the importance of personal confession and the necessity of dethroning your ego. These two steps are vitally important for being a true disciple and for fulfilling the Great Commission to make disciples for Christ.

> *"Heavenly Father, I don't want my ego to get in the way of seeing lost souls come to you. Please take away any legalism, impure thoughts, criticism, and anything else negative in my life so I can have compassion for the lost souls I encounter daily, Amen."*

Ending the Worship War

Read: John 4:19-24

This devotion encourages believers to focus on the core of worship, which is worshipping God in spirit and truth, rather than getting caught up in divisive debates over musical styles. It promotes understanding and appreciation for both traditional and contemporary forms of worship, emphasizing that unity in Christ is more important than differences in musical preference.

Did you know that for generations, the style of music in churches has caused separation in the body of Christ, with two different camps forming: traditional and contemporary. Many have strong opinions about their preferred style of worship, leading to the infamous *"worship war."* This divide has been a controversial topic throughout the history of the church. The battle rages on as younger generations favour contemporary music while seniors appreciate traditional hymns.

But beneath these comments and criticisms, there's a deeper issue:

people wish to have the kind of music they like or are familiar with. This longing is at the root of the problem, and many pastors struggle to address it effectively.

Efforts to please everyone can be challenging. Some churches host two services: one traditional and one contemporary, while others conduct them simultaneously in different locations. However, such approaches may not bridge the generational gap effectively and may even exacerbate the divide between youth and seniors.

This ongoing *"worship war"* is something Satan seems to relish, as the conflict has led to church closures and splits. This is why we need to address both young and old, fostering appreciation for each other's worship styles and understanding what God says about worship. Our goal is to apply these lessons to ensure that Satan does not gain a foothold in our worship ministry.

Addressing those who appreciate the hymns:

Traditional hymns often feature majestic, powerful lyrics that reflect the dignity of God. Lyrics like *"A Mighty Fortress is our God," "Blessed Assurance, Jesus is mine!"* They exalt the majesty of God.

Traditional hymns emotionally connect senior adults to a more stable and secure past. These songs have been a source of spiritual and emotional stability for many seniors, especially during significant life events.

Traditional hymns have ministered to seniors in times of great need, such as at funerals or during times of grief. Songs like *"In the Garden"* and *"Sweet By and By"* have served as spiritual markers in their lives.

We also need to know that our seniors have learned their theology through hymns. These songs cover essential theological concepts like redemption, security, salvation, and the Lordship of Christ. Singing these hymns helps them understand and internalize their faith.

Addressing those who appreciate Contemporary Worship:

Contemporary worship music is essential for reaching and embracing younger generations. Neglecting this style may lead to a decline in the church's youth attendance and involvement.

While traditional hymns sing about God, contemporary worship music often focuses on singing to God. This aligns with biblical principles that encourage believers to *"Sing to the Lord"* and *"Sing to Him."*

Our youth today are growing up in a rapidly changing world. They often lack confidence in their homes, government, and even the church. Scandals and instability have eroded their trust. However, when they encounter Jesus, they become passionate about their faith, and their music becomes their means of communication with Him.

Everyone needs to understand that the heart of worship is not the style but the sincerity and authenticity of the worshipper. Jesus emphasized this when He spoke to the Samaritan woman at the well, saying that true worshipers would worship in spirit and truth. The style of worship becomes irrelevant in light of this profound truth.

Differences in worship style are natural, but what unites us is our commitment to worship in spirit and truth. We should surrender our preferences and embrace both the old and the new. As we breathe together in worship, we exemplify the unity of the Body of Christ.

So, let us all take a breath together, set aside our differences in style, and worship our Lord in unity, thereby glorifying God as one body.

"Father, You desire that Your children worship You in unity. I pray that my preferences don't get in the way of that happening. My desire is to embrace both the old and the new so that more will come to know You as Lord and Saviour and that You will be glorified, Amen."

THE JOY OF THE LORD

Read: Isaiah 12:1-6

Scripture tells us to rejoice always, but what does that really look like in everyday life? Near the end of his life, Robert Louis Stevenson once said, "To miss the joy is to miss everything." That's a striking statement, especially from someone looking back over a lifetime. It reminds us how essential joy truly is.

I often tell people, *"Don't let anyone or anything rob you of your joy."* Yet, if we're honest, Christians are not always known as the most joyful people in the world. That should cause us to pause, because joy is something the enemy works hard to steal. Why? Because joy is contagious. Satan is content for people to go to heaven, but he does not want believers living in such a way that others desire what they have.

Joy is not meant to be rare in the Christian life. In fact, joy is a fruit produced by the Holy Spirit. (Galatians 5:22–23 NLT) tells us, *"But the Holy Spirit produces this kind of fruit in our lives: love, **joy**, peace,* *patience, kindness, goodness, faithfulness, gentleness, and self-control. There is no law against these things!"* Joy is not optional—it's evidence of God's Spirit at work within us.

Jesus made it very clear that fruitfulness flows from connection. In one of my life verses (John 15:5 NLT), He said, *"Anyone who remains in me and I in him will produce much fruit. For apart from me you can do nothing."* If we are truly connected to Jesus, joy should be visible in our lives to everyone else around us. As branches are joined to the life-giving vine, the fruit we bear should include joy.

It's also important to remember that this is not the *"fruit of the saints,"* but the fruit of the Spirit. Joy is not something we can manufacture through positive thinking or strong willpower. It comes from God. Apart from Christ, we can do nothing of eternal value.

There is, however, a difference between the joy of the world and the joy of the Lord. People often ask whether non-Christians can experience joy. The answer is yes—at least on a human or secular level. Because every person is made in the image of God, all people have the capacity to express love, kindness, patience, and even joy. Yet sin has distorted that image and broken our relationship with God, cutting us off from the true source of life.

Jesus came to restore that broken connection. When we are reconciled to God through Christ, the image of God within us begins to be restored. The fruit of the Spirit—including joy—is evidence that we have been reconnected to Him.

(Psalm 16:11 NLT) declares, *"You will show me the way of life, granting me the joy of your presence and the pleasures of living with you forever."* Complete joy is found in God's presence. This is not shallow happiness, but a deep, abiding joy that lacks nothing.

Human joy is temporary, like the happiness I previously stated. It's often tied to circumstances—celebrations, relationships, achievements, good health, or pleasant moments. While these are good gifts, they do not last. That is why happiness rises and falls with what happens to us. Human joy fades, but the joy of the Lord will endure forever.

Jesus demonstrated this difference clearly. On the night before His crucifixion, knowing He would soon be betrayed, beaten, and nailed to a cross, He said to His disciples, *"I have told you these things so that you will be filled with my joy. Yes, your joy will overflow!"* (John 15:11 NLT) Human joy would not survive such a moment, but the joy of the Lord did.

(Hebrews 12:2 NLT) reminds us that it was *"because of the joy awaiting him"* that Jesus endured the cross. Only spiritual, supernatural joy can stand firm in the face of suffering.

Everlasting joy belongs to those who have been redeemed by the Lord. (Romans 5:10–11 NLT) tells us that we have been restored to friendship with God through Jesus Christ, and because of that, *"We can rejoice in our wonderful new relationship with God."*

The key to experiencing this joy is intimacy with Jesus. If joy is lacking, the question is not whether Christ is sufficient, but whether we are truly connected to Him. Compromise weakens joy. Obedience strengthens it. When we remain in Christ, His life flows through us, and joy is the result.

We can experience the joy of the Lord on mountaintops and in valleys alike. James 1:2–4 tells us to consider it joy when trials come, because God is using them to mature and complete us. This kind of joy is only possible when we remain connected to the vine—Jesus Christ.

> *"Lord, I want to thank You for the joy that comes from knowing You. Forgive me for the times I have allowed circumstances, compromise, or distraction to rob me of that joy. Help me to remain closely connected to Jesus, the true vine, so that His life may flow through me, and may others be drawn to You through the joy they see in me. In Jesus' name I pray, Amen."*

Redeeming Value

Many countries today are actively reducing waste by recycling and implementing redemption programs. Bottles, cans, and other containers are collected and returned to redemption centres, where they are bought back and reused. The reason the maker of these bottles or cans is willing to redeem them is because they have redeeming value. They are not worthless; they can be restored and used again. This simple principle provides a helpful illustration for understanding God's redemptive plan for humanity.

Today's passage in Galatians 3 presents us with a spiritual crossroads. There are two paths before us: one is the way of the law, and the other is the way of faith. Paul writes that one road leads to a curse, and the other leads to a blessing.

Paul quotes from Leviticus 18:5 when he says that those who rely on the works of the law are under a curse (Galatians 3:10), because "*the law requires perfect obedience, and anyone who fails in even one point is guilty of breaking all of it"* (v10 NLT). The law, as given in the Old Testament, was primarily about doing—following rules and regulations. While it was holy and good, the law could not reach the heart or change the inner person. That is why Paul emphasizes that the law does not rest on faith (v12). The law cannot justify; it cannot make someone right before God. It simply exposes sin and shows our need for a Saviour.

Trying to earn righteousness by following the law is a tall order because it is all-or-nothing. (Deuteronomy 27:26 NLT) warns, *"Cursed is anyone who does not remain fully obedient to all the words of this law written in the Book of the Law."* The law reveals the standard, but no one can live up to it perfectly. It's like trying to pay off a mountain of debt with a single dollar—you'll never reach the top on your own.

The second road is the road of faith. Paul writes in (Galatians 3:11 NLT), *"The law is not based on faith. Instead, it says, 'The person who obeys these laws will live by them.'"* Faith calls us to trust God and His promises rather than our own efforts. Habakkuk reminds us, *"But the person who is righteous because of his faith will live"* (Habakkuk 2:4 NLT). Faith requires a daily walk, a daily reliance on God's grace, even when the path is difficult or countercultural.

Living by faith can be challenging in today's world. Modern culture often emphasizes tolerance, inclusivity, and relativism, and it can make the narrow biblical truth seem unkind or exclusive. Yet Jesus Himself declared, *"I am the way, the truth, and the life. No one can come to the Father except through me"* (John 14:6 NLT). Redemption, salvation, and the hope of eternal life are found only through Him.

To help understand this, consider a story from everyday life: imagine a teenager who accidentally breaks a neighbour's expensive window. The parents cannot repair it themselves, and the teenager certainly can't pay for it. Then the neighbour steps in and pays for the repair. That's redemption in action—a cost is paid because the item (or person) has value. Similarly, Christ paid the ultimate price for us. He took the penalty we deserved so we could be restored to God.

This road of faith leads to the blessing of redemption. Paul explains, *"Christ redeemed us from the curse of the law by becoming a curse for us, for it is written: 'Cursed is everyone who is hung on a tree.' He redeemed us in order that the blessing given to Abraham might come to the Gentiles through Christ Jesus, so that by faith we might receive the promised Holy Spirit"*

(Galatians 3:13-14, NLT). Like the redemption story in recycling or the broken window, Christ restored what was valuable: *us.*

As we reflect on this, let us consider our own path. Are we walking by sight, relying on our own efforts or worldly rules to earn God's approval? Or are we walking in the Spirit by faith, trusting in the redeeming power of Jesus Christ? Redemption is available, and God's Spirit is ready to guide us every step of the way. Choosing the road of faith allows us to experience God's blessing daily, even in the middle of life's challenges and uncertainties.

Our Maker paid the ultimate price for us because we are priceless to Him. Redemption is not just a concept; it's a reality we can experience today, in every choice we make and every step we take. May we choose wisely and live by faith, trusting that Christ's love and redemption are sufficient for every need, every failure, and every moment of doubt.

> *"Lord Jesus, your desire for me is to make wise choices and to live by faith daily. Help me to trust you completely, to rely on your redeeming power, and to walk in your ways so that I may experience the fullness of your blessing, Amen."*

DAY 14

ARE YOU RUNNING FOR GOD OR FROM GOD?

Read: Jonah 1:1-17

In the movie Chariots of Fire, Eric Liddell competed in the 400-meter race at the 1924 Olympics. Liddell was also slated to run the 100-meter race, but because the event was scheduled on a Sunday, he refused to compete. Even under intense pressure, he stood firm in his convictions. On the day of the 400-meter race, someone discreetly handed him a piece of paper that read, "Those who honour me I will honour" (1 Samuel 2:30, NLT). Clutching that verse in his hand, Eric ran his race with unwavering focus. Not only did he win the gold medal, but he also broke the existing world record with a time of 47.6 seconds. Eric had a passion for running, but his passion for God was stronger. He was clearly running for God, not from Him.

As believers, we too are running a race—the one God has set before us. Hebrews 12:1 reminds us, *"Therefore, since we are surrounded by such a huge crowd of witnesses to the life of faith, let us strip off every weight that slows us down, especially the sin that so easily trips us up. And let us run with endurance the race God has set before us."* But here's the question we must ask ourselves: are we running for God or from Him?

Sometimes God calls us to do things we don't want to do or to go places we'd rather avoid. This was Jonah's situation. God told him to go to Nineveh and preach repentance, but Jonah refused. Instead, he boarded a ship heading in the opposite direction, to Tarshish. Jonah's attempt to escape God is one of the clearest examples of running from Him in Scripture (Jonah 1:3, NLT).

Running from God is not a new phenomenon. Even in the Garden of Eden, Adam and Eve tried to hide from God. Genesis 3:8-10 says, *"Then the man and his wife heard the LORD God walking about in the garden in the cool of the day, and they hid from the LORD God among the trees. But the LORD God called to the man, 'Where are you?' He replied, 'I heard you walking in the garden, so I hid. I was afraid because I was naked.'"* Sin, fear, and shame often make us run and hide, just as they did with Adam and Eve.

So, if you find yourself running from God today, pause and ask: Where are you running to? Like Jonah, people often flee to the most unlikely places when they are trying to escape God. Jonah bought a ticket to Tarshish, yet even in his flight, his mind and heart were unsettled. When we run from God, we often make irrational decisions, avoid the counsel of family and friends, and distance ourselves from sources of wisdom and support—including our church community.

But here is the good news: you cannot outrun God. Jonah tried, but it didn't work. God knows where you are, even if it feels like you are in the belly of a whale. God may even allow circumstances to discipline or redirect us, just as He did with Jonah. Sometimes, the storm comes, the ship rocks, and our world feels chaotic, but it's all part of God's loving effort to get our attention and draw us back to Him.

An illustration to consider is a child running through a crowded park, trying to hide from a parent. No matter how fast the child runs, eventually the parent will catch up because of love and care. In the same way, God's pursuit of us is relentless and motivated by His love. When we finally stop running and turn toward Him, we experience restoration, peace, and purpose.

The challenge for us is clear: when life gets tough, run to God, not away from Him. When you feel pressure, stress, or fear, surrender to

Him rather than running on your own strength. Choose to trust Him and obey, because hiding will never give you freedom, but running for God will lead you to victory and blessing.

Just as Eric Liddell ran with his eyes on God, we are called to run our spiritual race with faith, courage, and endurance. Our race is not about avoiding challenges—it's about staying close to God, listening to His voice, and walking the path He has set for us, no matter how difficult it may seem.

"Lord, I don't want to run from you; I want to run for you. Give me the strength, courage, and endurance to run this race faithfully. Help me to surrender my fears, listen to your voice, and follow the path you have set before me, Amen."

A Lesson From the Ants

The Bible tells us to "Go to the ant, you sluggard; consider its ways and be wise!" (Proverbs 6:6 NLT) One sunny afternoon, I was in my yard, captivated as I watched ants coming and going from their anthill. Each ant moved with focus and determination, carrying food, coordinating with others, and never seeming to pause. Curious, I did a little research and discovered some fascinating facts. There are over 10,000 species of ants, and some can lift 20 times their own body weight. They can build structures 500 times their own height, and even though their brains are tiny, they contain roughly 250,000 cells. Amazingly, ants have two stomachs—one for themselves and another for storing food to share with others. Isn't God's creation amazing?

There is much we can learn from these small creatures, beginning with performance. Unlike humans, ants work in harmony, each knowing their role and responsibility. They focus on their goal and don't fight among themselves. Scripture instructs us to do the same: "*Whatever you do, do it enthusiastically, as something done for the Lord and not for men*" (Ecclesiastes 9:10 NLT), and "*Whatever you do or say, do it as a representative of the Lord Jesus, giving thanks through him to God the Father*" (Colossians 3:17 NLT). Like the ants, when we are diligent, focused, and committed, we can accomplish much even when we feel small or inadequate. (Psalm 133:1 NLT) reminds us, "*How wonderful, how pleasant, when brothers live together in harmony!*"

The second lesson is partnership. My research revealed that on their own, each ant's work seems insignificant. But when swarms of ants come together, they organize naturally, achieving tasks far beyond the ability of any single ant. In the same way, God calls us to partner with others in the body of Christ. Each believer has unique gifts and abilities, and when we work together in service, prayer, encouragement, or teaching, we accomplish far more than we could alone. The unity of believers strengthens the entire community, just as ants strengthen their colony.

Preparedness is another quality we learn from ants. (Proverbs 6:8 NLT) says, "*Ants are creatures of little strength, yet they store up their food in the summer.*" Even though an ant's lifespan is only 45–60 days, it works diligently while the weather is warm to store food for the future. Many of the ants that gather food will never personally consume it; they work for the next generation. In the same way, God calls us to prepare the next generation of Christians by mentoring, teaching, and setting examples of faith, diligence, and integrity. What we do today can bless generations to come.

Finally, ants teach us perseverance. They don't quit when obstacles arise, and if their colony is destroyed, they rebuild quickly and continue working. Christians are also called to persevere. (James 1:2-4 NLT) says, "*Dear brothers and sisters, when troubles come your way, consider it an opportunity for great joy. For you know that when your faith is tested, your endurance has a chance to grow. So let it grow, for when your endurance is fully developed, you will be mature and complete, needing nothing.*"

Today, let us consider the ant because we are called to perform the task God has for us, and as we do, we must partner with others. We are also called to prepare the next generation of Christians and to persevere in our faith until God calls us home.

"Lord, thank you for this lesson from the ants. Their lives have taught me today that I want my performance, partnership, preparedness, and perseverance to glorify you. Teach me today how to be stronger in these areas of my life, Amen."

"Lord, thank you for this lesson from the ants. Their lives have taught me today that I want my performance, partnership, preparedness, and perseverance to glorify you. Teach me today how to be stronger in these areas of my life, Amen."

FOCUSSING ON HEAVEN

Read: John 14:1-11

A retiring missionary couple once arrived in New York City after many years of faithful service overseas. As they stepped off the ship, they saw bands playing and crowds cheering. The husband assumed the celebration was for them, honouring their long obedience in the mission field. But soon they discovered the truth: President Theodore Roosevelt had been on the same ship, returning from a hunting expedition, and the fanfare was for him.

That night, deeply discouraged, the missionary said to his wife, *"I can't take this. God is not treating us fairly."* Gently, she replied, *"Why don't you go into the bedroom and tell that to the Lord?"* After a short while, he returned with a peaceful expression. When his wife asked what had happened, he said, *"I told the Lord how discouraged I was about returning home, and He reminded me that I'm not home yet."*

That simple reminder captures a truth we often forget: this world is not our home. In (John 14:1–3 NLT), Jesus speaks tenderly to His disciples on the night before His crucifixion: *"Don't let your hearts be troubled. Trust in God, and trust also in me. There is more than enough room in my Father's home... I am going to prepare a place for you."* Jesus was lifting their eyes beyond the coming pain to the promise of heaven. Earth was never meant to be the final destination for God's people.

Jesus goes on to say, *"When everything is ready, I will come and get you, so that you will always be with me where I am"* (John 14:3 NLT). Heaven is not just a place—it is a promise of eternal fellowship with Christ. For believers, the best is always yet to come.

Scripture gives us glimpses of what awaits us in heaven. We are told there will be singing and worship before God's throne (Revelation 15:3; Psalm 148:2). Heaven will be a place of rest from our struggle, persecution, and weariness. Paul writes that God will give *"rest to you who are suffering"* (2 Thessalonians 1:7 NLT). Revelation assures us there will be no hunger, no thirst, and no more tears, because God Himself will wipe every tear from our eyes (Revelation 7:16–17 NLT).

Keeping our hearts focused on heaven requires discipline. It does not come naturally, especially when life is difficult. As believers, we are engaged in a spiritual battle, and like soldiers, we must stay prepared. I served my country for nearly twenty years, and each day began the same way—getting up, getting dressed, and preparing for duty. You could not step into battle unprepared.

In the same way, Christians are called to live with readiness. Jeremiah says, *"Prepare your shields, and advance into battle!"* (Jeremiah 46:3 NLT) Paul echoes this truth in (Ephesians 6:11 NLT): *"Put on all of God's armour so that you will be able to stand firm against all strategies of the devil."* Until our mission on earth is complete, we must live alert, faithful, and focused on the eternal reward.

When the fight becomes intense and discouragement sets in, Scripture offers comfort. *"He ransoms me and keeps me safe from the battle waged against me"* (Psalm 55:18 NLT). God sees every struggle. None of our faithfulness will go unnoticed. One day, every sacrifice will be worth it.

The promise of heaven is not automatic—it's personal. Scripture teaches clearly that eternal life is given to those who place their faith in Jesus Christ. *"If you openly declare that Jesus is Lord and believe in your heart that God raised him from the dead, you will be saved"* (Romans 10:9 NLT). Verse 11 adds, *"Anyone who trusts in him will never be disgraced."*

Heaven belongs to those who belong to Christ.

If you have never trusted Jesus as your Saviour, today can be the day of salvation. Call upon His name, believe in Him, and receive the promise of eternal life. And if you already belong to Him, take heart—no matter how unnoticed or weary your journey feels, you are not home yet. Keep your eyes fixed on heaven.

"Jesus, I thank You for the promise and invitation of heaven. When this world weighs heavily on my heart, help me remember that my true home is with You. Strengthen me to live as a faithful soldier— alert, obedient, and focused on eternity. Give me courage to fight the good fight and grace to finish well until the day comes when You will call me home. In Jesus' mighty name, I ask these things, Amen."

From Slavery to Sonship

Read: Galatians 4:1-7

Paul wrote his letter to the Galatians to address a serious spiritual danger—legalism. Legalism can look impressive. It can sound disciplined, mature, and deeply committed to God. But in reality, it is empty and powerless. Legalism focuses on rules rather than relationships and on performance rather than grace. It gives the appearance of progress while missing the true destination altogether.

Imagine a pilot standing before his passengers and saying, "*Folks, I have good news and bad news. The bad news is that our navigator has lost our position and we've been flying aimlessly for over an hour. But the good news is—we're making great time.*" No one would be comforted by that announcement. Speed is meaningless without direction. Legalism is much the same. It can be very busy, very strict, and very serious—yet completely lost. It's like flying without a flight plan.

This was the problem in Galatia. The believers there had begun to think that strict adherence to the Law would somehow make them better Christians. They believed maturity was found in rules and rituals rather than in Christ. Paul reminds them firmly and lovingly that they are no longer slaves to the Law but are now children of God.

In Galatians 4:4–7, Paul reveals the unique and beautiful relationship believers now have with the Lord. He writes, *"But when the set time had fully come, God sent his Son…to redeem those under the law, that we might receive adoption to sonship"* (vv. 4–5, NIV). God sent His Son with a purpose—to buy our freedom and bring us into His family. Redemption was never the end goal; adoption was.

This idea of being called God's children would have been shocking to Paul's readers. In the Old Testament, God's people were rarely referred to as His children in a personal sense. Yet even then, God hinted at what was to come. Through the prophet Hosea, God said, *"In the place where it was said to them, 'You are not my people,' they will be called 'children of the living God'"* (Hosea 1:10 NIV). What was once a promise has now become a reality. The apostle John later declared with awe, *"See what great love the Father has lavished on us, that we should be called children of God! And that is what we are!"* (1 John 3:1 NIV).

We are God's children because we have been adopted by Him. Adoption is not accidental or reluctant—it is intentional and costly. The Galatians were no longer held captive to the Law because Jesus paid the price to redeem them. God did not free them only to leave them on their own; He freed them so He could bring them home. Paul says that because of this adoption, God has sent *"the Spirit of his Son into our hearts, the Spirit who calls out, 'Abba, Father'"* (Galatians 4:6 NIV). We don't relate to God as fearful slaves, but as beloved children who can call Him *"Father."*

God's desire for His adopted children is not that they strive to earn His love, but that they live in gratitude for the grace they have already received. Legalism forgets the gift. Sonship celebrates it.

Finally, Paul reminds us that adoption also makes us heirs. *"So you are no longer a slave, but God's child; and since you are his child, God has made you also an heir"* (Galatians 4:7 NIV). Elsewhere, Paul writes, *"Now if we are children, then we are heirs—heirs of God and co-heirs with Christ"* (Romans 8:17 NIV).

There is a story of a young boy hired to work on a neglected farm. The buildings were run down, and the land was in poor condition, but he thought to himself, "*This isn't my place.*" One evening, the elderly couple who owned the farm invited him to dinner. They shared how much he had meant to them, and since they had no children, they asked him to become their heir. He accepted with gratitude. Within weeks, his attitude completely changed. Repairs were made, improvements began, and care was taken. Why? Because it was no longer just a place where he worked—it was now his inheritance. Though not born into the family, he had all the rights of a real son.

That is the difference between slavery and sonship. Christians are no longer slaves striving to earn approval. They are children of God—adopted by grace and made heirs of the Kingdom. When we truly understand who we are, it will change how we live.

"Father, thank You that I am no longer a slave but Your child. Thank You for adopting me into Your family and making me an heir of Your Kingdom. Help me to never take Your grace for granted. Teach me to live each day with gratitude, humility, and confidence in Your love. I am thankful to call You my Father, Amen."

No Hope, False Hope, True Hope

Read: Titus 2:11-15

Faith and hope in the Bible are closely connected, yet they are not the same. Understanding the difference between them is essential to living a Spirit-led life. Faith is something believers possess, strengthen, and actively exercise. Faith trusts God and responds to His Word in obedience. James tells us that trials test our faith and help it grow stronger as we learn to persevere (James 1:2–4 NKJV). Faith moves us to action.

Hope, however, works alongside faith. Hope cheers faith on. Faith reaches out and accepts the promises of God. At the same time, hope looks ahead with confident expectation that those promises will be fulfilled. Faith says, "*God has spoken,*" and hope says, "*God will surely do what He has promised.*" Without hope, faith can become weary, and without faith, hope has no foundation.

In Titus 2:12–13, Paul teaches that the grace of God instructs us "*that, denying ungodliness and worldly lusts, we should live soberly, righ-*

teously, and godly in the present age, looking for the blessed hope and glorious appearing of our great God and Saviour Jesus Christ" (NKJV). The word *"hope"* here comes from the Greek elpida, meaning confident expectation. Biblical hope is not wishful thinking or positive optimism—it is a settled confidence in what God has promised. As believers, we live with our eyes fixed on the coming day when Christ will be revealed in glory and we will dwell with Him forever.

Many people in this world live with no hope. Paul reminded the Ephesians that before they came to Christ, they were *"without Christ... having no hope and without God in the world"* (Ephesians 2:12 NKJV). Life apart from Christ may appear full, busy, or successful, but spiritually it is empty and directionless. To live without Christ is to live without eternal hope. This truth should stir our hearts and compel us to lovingly share the message of salvation with those who are lost. Let us also examine ourselves honestly. Are we truly confident in our eternal destiny? If we are unsure, that uncertainty must be settled. True hope begins with a right relationship with God through Jesus Christ.

Even more concerning than having no hope is living with false hope. Jesus warned about this danger in Matthew 7:21–27. He spoke of people who believed they were secure because of religious words and outward actions. Yet, their lives were not built on obedience to Him. These individuals stand before Christ with confidence, only to discover that their hope was misplaced. Jesus compared them to a foolish man who built his house on sand. When the storms came, everything collapsed. False hope is deceptive because it feels safe—until it is too late. Before someone can embrace true biblical hope, they must first be willing to admit that their false hope cannot save them.

Christians, however, are called to live in and proclaim true hope. True hope is anchored in the finished work of Christ and focused on His return. Take time to read Titus 2:13 through 3:7, and personalize the passage by replacing *"we"* and *"us"* with *"me."* Doing so reminds us that this hope is not abstract—it's deeply personal. True hope shapes how we live today. It teaches us to say no to sin and yes to godly living, not out of fear, but out of gratitude for grace.

Those who possess true hope live with confidence, because this hope is secure. The writer of Hebrews tells us that this hope is *"an anchor of the soul, both sure and steadfast"* (Hebrews 6:19 NKJV). In a world of uncertainty, shifting values, and broken promises, our hope holds firm.

It anchors us through the storms of life and draws us closer to God's presence.

Finally, believers are called not only to live with true hope but to share it. We are to honour Christ as Lord in our hearts and be ready to give an answer to anyone who asks about the hope that is within us (1 Peter 3:15 NKJV). The question remains: are you living with true hope, and are you prepared to share that hope with others who are searching for something real?

> *"Lord Jesus, I want to be someone who not only possesses true hope, but lives confidently in it every day. Anchor my soul in Your promises, guard me from false hope, and give me boldness and compassion to share the hope I have in You with others, Amen."*

The What, Why, and How of Worship

Read: Psalm 95:1-7

Renowned preacher A.W. Tozer once said, "Worship is the missing jewel of the church." Another well-known observation adds, "We have become a generation of people who worship our work, work at our play, and play at our worship." (Charles "Chuck" Swindoll) Those words are both sobering and revealing. They force us to pause and ask an important question: What is biblical worship really meant to be?

To answer that question, we can explore worship from three simple yet profound angles—the what, the why, and the how of worship.

Let's begin with the what of worship. Sometimes it helps to understand something by first recognizing what it is not. Worship is not a music event, a concert, or a performance designed to impress others. It is not dependent on musical style, volume, or emotional atmosphere. Worship is also not merely a feeling, though feelings may accompany it. Jesus addressed this kind of empty outward worship when He said,

"These people honour me with their lips, but their hearts are far from me" (Matthew 15:8 NIV).

Authentic worship always begins in the heart. It is an expression of love and devotion toward God that flows from a genuine relationship with Him. Scripture reminds us, *"We love because he first loved us"* (1 John 4:19 NIV). Because God has loved us, called us, saved us, and continually provides for us, we respond by declaring His worth. Worship, at its core, is recognizing who God is and responding appropriately—with gratitude, humility, and reverence.

Next, let's consider the why of worship. Why do we worship God at all? Psalm 95 gives us a clear answer. We worship God because of who He is, and we praise Him in response to what He has done. *"For the Lord is the great God, the great King above all gods"* (Psalm 95:3 NIV). He is our Creator, our Sustainer, and the Rock of our salvation.

Psalm 95 also reminds us that God is not distant or harsh, but personal and caring. *"For he is our God and we are the people of his pasture, the flock under his care"* (Psalm 95:7, NIV). This beautiful image helps us understand our relationship with Him. He is the Shepherd; we are the sheep. He is the Creator; we are His creation. He is the King; we are His subjects. He is the Master; we are His servants. Because of this, He alone is worthy of our worship. We worship Jesus because He is our Saviour, and we praise Him because we belong to Him.

Finally, let's explore the how of worship. Worship can be deeply personal and private, but it is also meant to be shared and expressed corporately. Psalm 95 repeatedly uses the phrase *"let us,"* reminding us that worship is something we do together as God's people. *"Come, let us sing for joy to the Lord… let us come before him with thanksgiving… let us bow down in worship, let us kneel before the Lord our Maker"* (Psalm 95:1–6 NIV).

Worship also involves both our attitudes and our actions. Scripture shows us that physical expressions of worship can reflect inward devotion. We can bow and kneel before God in humility. We can clap our hands and shout for joy (Psalm 47:1). We can lift our hands in praise and bless the Lord (Psalm 134:2). These actions are not performances—they are responses of a heart that recognizes God's greatness.

Ultimately, worship is far more than singing on Sundays. It is a lifestyle. True worship means continually placing God first in what we say, think, and do. When we gather to sing, we are simply putting music to the song that is already being written in our hearts throughout the week. Our daily obedience, surrender, and gratitude become acts of worship that honour God just as much as any song.

"Lord, I desire to worship You in spirit and in truth. I don't want my worship to be empty words or routine actions. Shape my heart so that my attitudes and actions reflect genuine praise for who You are. Teach me to live a life of worship, placing You first in all I do because You alone are worthy, Amen."

Is Sunday Still A Holy Day?

Read: Exodus 20:8-11

Is Sunday still holy, or has it become just another ordinary day of the week? David L. Herring once observed, "Our great-grandfathers called Sunday the Holy Sabbath; our grandfathers called it the Sabbath; our fathers called it Sunday; but today people simply call it the weekend." That statement may sound humorous, but it reveals a serious spiritual drift. What was once treated as sacred has gradually become casual, convenient, and often optional.

In Exodus 20:8–11, God commands His people, "*Remember to observe the Sabbath day by keeping it holy.*" While this passage is rooted in the Old Testament law, it reveals an unchanging principle about God's design for our lives. God set aside one day as different—distinct from the others—not as a burden, but as a blessing.

Although we are reading from the Old Testament, the New Testament repeatedly affirms the importance of gathering regularly with

God's people. Dwight L. Moody once said, "*Church attendance is as vital to a disciple as a transfusion of rich, healthy blood to a sick man.*" In the early church, believers began observing the Lord's Day rather than the Jewish Sabbath, because Sunday marked the resurrection of Jesus Christ. While the day changed, the reverence did not. They treated the Lord's Day as holy, setting it apart for worship, fellowship, and spiritual renewal. If that is true, then we must ask ourselves why Sunday should still matter to us today.

One important reason is rest. God designed us with limits. In Exodus 20:9–10, the Lord says we are to labour for six days, but the seventh day is to be set aside for rest. Work itself is not the problem—Scripture affirms the value of diligence and responsibility. Paul writes, "*Those unwilling to work will not get to eat*" (2 Thessalonians 3:10 NLT), and elsewhere we are reminded that providing for our families matters deeply to God (1 Timothy 5:8).

God's command to rest was never meant to rob us of joy or productivity. Instead, it was intended to protect our physical, emotional, and spiritual health. God knew a time would come when people would live to work rather than work to live. Setting aside Sunday as a holy day reminds us that our worth is not measured by our output, and our lives are sustained by God, not by endless activity.

Another reason Sunday remains holy is reflection. Exodus 20:8 tells us to remember and observe. God Himself modelled reflection when He looked upon His completed creation and declared it good. Sunday gives us a sacred pause—a moment to look back over the past week and recognize God's hand at work.

It is a day when we are encouraged not to neglect meeting together as believers (Hebrews 10:25 NLT). As we gather, we reflect on God's faithfulness, His provision, and His promises. We remember that wherever we go, God is with us: "*Be sure of this: I am with you always*" (Matthew 28:20 NLT). We reflect on the assurance that God will never leave us nor abandon us (Hebrews 13:5). We are reminded that whatever needs we face, "*God will supply all your needs*" (Philippians 4:19), and whatever challenges lie ahead, Christ will give us strength (Philippians 4:13).

Finally, Sunday is a powerful opportunity to renew our commitment to God. Each week, we are shaped by the pressures, values, and distractions of this world. Sunday invites us to realign our hearts and minds. As Paul writes, "*Don't copy the behaviour and customs of this world, but let God transform you into a new person by changing the way you think"* (Romans 12:2 NLT).

When we gather on Sundays, we worship, examine our hearts, confess our sins, and recommit ourselves to following Christ in the coming week. It becomes a spiritual reset—a reminder that we belong to God and live for His purposes.

So, is Sunday still a holy day? The answer is yes. For the Christian, Sunday remains a sacred gift from God—a day to rest, reflect, and renew. It's a special time when we come together in worship, celebration, and spiritual examination. May we resist the temptation to treat it casually and instead receive it gratefully.

> *"Lord, help me to honour Sundays as a gift from You. Teach me to use this day to rest my body, reflect on Your faithfulness, and renew my commitment to You. Guard my heart from treating what is holy as common, and draw me closer to You as I gather with Your people, Amen."*

From Awe to Amazing

Read: Psalm 19-1-6

In the vast tapestry of creation, God meticulously crafted the universe long before placing humanity at the forefront of His masterpiece. Scripture tells us that God created the heavens, the earth, the sun and moon, the seas, and every living creature before He formed mankind in His own image (Genesis 1:1–26). Creation was not rushed or accidental—it was intentional, ordered, and then declared "very good."

Yet we live in a world increasingly enamoured with the idea that everything came into being by chance. Scientific theories of evolution are often presented as explanations that leave no room for God. This creates an apparent collision between scientific narratives and biblical faith. The question many people wrestle with is this: Can the intricate design of life truly coexist with the idea of randomness, or does creation itself point unmistakably to a Creator?

When we peer into the microscopic world of molecular biology, we encounter staggering complexity. Cells are not simple blobs of matter; they function like miniature cities, complete with communication systems, energy producers, repair mechanisms, and information storage. Carl Sagan once asserted that evolution is a fact supported by the fossil record and molecular biology. Yet even Charles Darwin acknowledged a significant weakness in his own theory. He admitted that if a complex organ existed that could not be formed by *"numerous, successive, slight modifications,"* then his theory would break down.

In 1953, the discovery of DNA dramatically reshaped our understanding of life. What Darwin assumed to be simple cells were revealed to contain vast amounts of coded information—more sophisticated than any man-made system. DNA operates like a language, conveying instructions with remarkable accuracy. As scientific knowledge has expanded, many researchers have begun to question whether such precision could truly arise without intelligent design.

Consider a watch. Every tiny gear serves a purpose, and if one piece is missing or malfunctioning, the watch fails. No one would argue that a watch assembled itself over time through random processes. In the same way, the extraordinary complexity of the cell has led even prominent scientists to admit that traditional evolutionary explanations fall short. Dr. Francis Crick, one of the co-discoverers of DNA, eventually proposed *"Directed Panspermia"*—the idea that life may have been seeded on Earth by extraterrestrial intelligence. Rather than acknowledging God, some theories simply move the problem elsewhere.

The fossil record also raises important questions. Darwin himself confessed that the geological record did not reveal the smooth, gradual progression his theory required. Even today, many evolutionary scientists admit that the fossil evidence does not clearly demonstrate the transitional forms needed to fully support evolution. While interpretations vary, the absence of definitive proof leaves room—significant room—for faith.

Against this backdrop of uncertainty and debate, the Bible speaks with clarity and confidence: *"The heavens declare the glory of God; and the firmament shows His handiwork"* (Psalm 19:1 NKJV). Creation does not whisper—it declares. The vastness of the universe, the beauty of a sunrise, the precision of the stars in their courses, and the intricacy of human life all point beyond themselves to a glorious Creator.

Psalm 19 reminds us that creation communicates God's greatness without words. Day after day and night after night, the heavens testify to His power and wisdom. When we lift our eyes to the sky or reflect on the complexity of life within us, we are invited to move from awe to something deeper—worship, trust, and surrender.

God did not merely create the universe and step away. The same God who designed the cosmos also formed us with intention and purpose. He knows us, redeems us, and has plans for our lives that are just as intricate as the world He spoke into existence. What begins as awe at creation should lead us to amazement at God's personal care and redemptive love.

As we contemplate the wonders around us, may our hearts overflow with gratitude. Creation reminds us that our lives are not accidents and our faith is not misplaced. The God who crafted the heavens is the same God who holds our future.

> *"Lord, when I consider the work of Your hands, I am filled with awe. The realization that You, in Your infinite wisdom, designed this universe—and lovingly created and redeemed me—leaves me humbled and grateful. Help me move from awe to a deeper amazement at who You are and what You are doing in my life, and may the wonders of Your creation continually draw my heart to worship You, Amen."*

DAY 22

BLESSINGS COME BY FAITH

Read: Galatians 3:1-9

One Christmas, we purchased a GPS. Its purpose was simple—to get us to our destination. If we missed a turn or wandered off course, it would patiently recalculate and guide us back onto the right road. But there was one condition: we had to trust it. If we ignored its directions or insisted on going our own way, we would only become more lost.

In Galatians 3, we discover that the believers in Galatia had taken a wrong turn spiritually. They needed to be rerouted. Paul's words to them are sharp and direct: *"You foolish Galatians! Who has bewitched you?"* (Galatians 3:1 NIV) His concern was not cruelty but care. They had started well, but somewhere along the journey, they had lost their focus and drifted off course. Like travellers ignoring their GPS, they were heading in the wrong direction.

Paul begins by telling them to look to the cross. He reminds them that Jesus Christ was clearly portrayed as crucified before their very eyes (v.1). In other words, the message of the cross was presented to them so vividly that it was as if they had personally witnessed it. Paul wanted them to return to the foundation of their faith—to remember why Christ died and what His sacrifice accomplished.

When Paul called them *"foolish,"* he was not insulting their intelligence. The Greek word he used means *"spiritually dull."* They had allowed something essential to fade from view. Taking our focus off the cross is like ignoring our GPS. When we stop trusting in Christ's finished work and start relying on ourselves, we wander aimlessly. As James T. Dyet observed *in Let My People Go,* *"There was a time when the Galatians first looked in faith to the cross. They gladly accepted the one who died on the cross as their Lord and Saviour. Sometime later, however, they took their eyes off Calvary and focused them on men. Men who minimized the adequate sacrifice of Christ on the cross by insisting on adding Mosaic law to faith in Christ as a means of justification."*

Paul then urges them to look to the Spirit. He asks a series of probing questions: *"Did you receive the Spirit by the works of the law, or by believing what you heard?"* (Galatians 3:2 NIV) The answer was obvious. They received the Holy Spirit not through rule-keeping, but through faith in Christ. Paul presses the point further: *"After beginning by means of the Spirit, are you now trying to finish by means of the flesh?"* (v.3).

The Christian life does not begin by faith and continue by human effort alone. The same Spirit who saves us also sustains us. He convicts us, guides us, strengthens us, leads us, and transforms us as we yield to Him. When we attempt to grow spiritually through sheer determination or religious performance, we move away from dependence on God and toward self-reliance. Staying focused on the Spirit keeps us aligned with God's direction and power.

Finally, Paul tells the Galatians to look to the Scriptures. He points them back to Abraham, reminding them that, *"Abraham believed God, and it was credited to him as righteousness"* (Galatians 3:6, NIV). Long before the law was given, God established a pattern—righteousness comes through faith. Paul explains that those who have faith are the true children of Abraham and that Scripture itself foresaw that God would justify the Gentiles by faith (vv. 7–9).

This was not a new idea; it was God's plan all along. The promise of blessing was never tied to law-keeping, but to trusting God's Word. Faith has always been the pathway to blessing.

Listen closely, my Christian friend. Every day we must intentionally look to the cross, be led by the Spirit, and remain grounded in the Scriptures. These are God's means of keeping us on course. When we trust in God's plan with a right heart, our faith is strengthened, and our lives are aligned with God's will.

> *"Lord Jesus, help me to keep my eyes fixed on the cross, my heart yielded to Your Spirit, and my life anchored in Your Word. May they be my daily guide, keeping me faithful, fruitful, and focused on You. I trust You to lead me, and I thank You for the blessings that come by faith, Amen."*

It's Time to Wake Up, Get Dressed, and Go to Work

Read: Romans 13:11-14

Sometimes sleeping in is not a great idea. During my years serving in the military, I learned that lesson quickly. In fact, I slept in once—and only once. In my nineteen-year career, I served with some outstanding men and women, but a few struggled to wake up on time. That lack of readiness didn't just affect them personally; it impacted their duties and those around them. When it comes to responsibility, being asleep at the wrong time can have serious consequences.

In Romans 13:11–14, the Apostle Paul delivers a similar wake-up call to believers. In essence, he tells them it's time to wake up, get dressed, and get to work. Paul's words are urgent and practical, reminding Christians that spiritual drowsiness is dangerous in a world that desperately needs the light of Christ.

Paul begins by saying, *"This is all the more urgent, for you know how late it is; time is running out*" (Romans 13:11 NLT). He draws attention to two things: time and sleep. Time is short, and sleep—spiritual sleep—can be costly. This sleep may refer to sin, spiritual apathy, or inactivity, and often these issues are closely connected. You see, when believers grow careless about their sin, they also tend to drift away from faithful obedience.

Throughout this chapter, Paul instructs believers on how to live responsibly, including submitting to governing authorities—even when those authorities are far from ideal. The Roman Christians were living under the rule of Nero, yet Paul reminded them that all authority ultimately derives from God. Jesus Himself taught His followers not to rebel against the government but to live in a way that honours God (Luke 23:13–16). Obedience, humility, and faithfulness are not optional for believers—they are part of staying spiritually awake.

Paul frequently addresses the seriousness of sin in his letters. One scholar notes that Paul uses the Greek word for "*sin*" dozens of times, especially in Romans. Sin disrupts our fellowship with God and robs us of peace. Scripture says, "*There is no health in my body because of my sins. There is no rest for my bones*" (Psalm 38:3 NLT). When Christians sin, rest disappears, conviction sets in, and spiritual sleep becomes restless and heavy.

After calling believers to wake up, Paul says it's time to clean up. "*The night is almost gone; the day of salvation will soon be here. So remove your dark deeds like dirty clothes, and put on the shining armour of right living*" (Romans 13:12 NLT). The imagery here is powerful. Night represents sin and moral darkness, while day symbolizes salvation, holiness, and truth.

After a long day in the Army, I often came home filthy. The first thing I did was shed my dirty clothes. Paul uses this same picture to describe repentance. Sin must be taken off—it cannot simply be covered up or ignored. We are called to intentionally remove sinful habits, attitudes, and behaviours that no longer belong to us.

But Paul doesn't stop there. After telling us to take off what is dirty, he instructs us to get dressed. We are to clothe ourselves with right living, walking openly and honourably as people of the light. If we want to resist sin, obey Christ, and serve faithfully, we must be properly dressed for spiritual work.

Paul refers to this clothing as the "*armour of light.*" This is not casual attire—it's battle gear. The Christian life is not lived on neutral ground. The enemy will do everything possible to distract, discourage, and derail believers from doing the Lord's work. That is why Paul later urges Christians to *"put on all of God's armour so that you will be able to stand firm against all strategies of the devil"* (Ephesians 6:11 NLT). He also reminds believers to put on the new self, created to be like God in true righteousness and holiness (Ephesians 4:24).

To wake up, clean up, and get dressed is to live alert, repentant, and prepared. God has work for us to do, and He supplies everything we need to do it well.

> *"Jesus, help me to stay spiritually awake and alert. Cleanse my heart from anything that doesn't honour You, and clothe me in righteousness so I am ready for service. Create in me a clean heart and use my life for Your purposes and Your glory today, Amen."*

DAY 24

CONTROLLING OUR ANGER

Read: Ephesians 4:26-31

How do we deal with our anger biblically, especially when Scripture tells us, "Don't sin by letting anger control you. Don't let the sun go down while you are still angry" (Ephesians 4:26 NLT)? This is not just a helpful suggestion from the apostle Paul—it is a loving warning. Unchecked anger has consequences, and today we want to explore how God calls us to handle it.

Anger is something we all experience. For some of us, it surfaces quickly and loudly; for others, it simmers quietly beneath the surface. As a teenager, I struggled deeply with anger, especially while playing sports. I remember kicking ball returns in the bowling alley and throwing golf clubs across the course. I might have brushed it off as being competitive or *"just a bad sport,"* but the truth is I was harbouring anger that I didn't know how to control. Looking back, I see clearly what Paul teaches us here—uncontrolled anger is not harmless; it's sinful and destructive.

That said, the Bible also shows us that not all anger is sinful. There is such a thing as righteous or sinless anger. Jesus Himself demonstrated this when He entered the Temple courtyard and overturned the tables of the money changers. His anger was never selfish or impulsive; it was always directed toward injustice and sin that dishonoured God and harmed others. Righteous anger is not about defending our pride or getting our way—it is about valuing God's holiness and the well-being of people above ourselves. Paul echoes this mindset when he writes, *"Don't be selfish; don't try to impress others. Be humble, thinking of others as better than yourselves"* (Philippians 2:3–4 NLT).

Paul instructs the believers in Ephesus to get a handle on their anger before it gets a handle on them. He writes, *"If you are angry, do not sin by nursing your grudge. Don't let the sun go down while you are still angry"* (Ephesians 4:26 NLT). The warning here is clear: anger itself may arise, but allowing it to linger, grow, and fester opens the door to sin. Unresolved anger has a way of settling into our hearts, shaping our attitudes, and influencing our actions in ways we often don't realize.

It is helpful to remember that in Paul's day, a new day began when the sun went down, not when it rose. This means his instruction was even more urgent than it might first appear. Paul urges believers to address anger quickly and decisively. Regardless of how we mark the beginning of a new day, the principle remains the same: anger should not be carried over into tomorrow. When we allow anger to remain, it hardens into resentment, and resentment can easily turn into bitterness. Scripture reminds us, *"People with a hot temper do foolish things"* (Proverbs 14:17a NLT). How many regrets, broken relationships, and careless words can be traced back to moments when anger was left unchecked?

Paul goes on to warn that unresolved anger creates a spiritual vulnerability: *"For anger gives a foothold to the devil"* (Ephesians 4:27 NLT). This is sobering. When we cling to anger, we are not simply dealing with an emotional issue; we are engaging in a spiritual battle. The enemy delights in using anger to divide relationships, damage our witness, and pull our hearts away from Christ. What begins as a moment of frustration can quickly become a tool the devil uses to disrupt our peace and effectiveness as believers.

Paul's advice in verses 29 and 30 will allow us to redirect and redeem our anger. He tells us that our words should be an encouragement and that our speech should be wholesome, edifying each other and the church. The word *"abusive"* in verse 29 means *"corrupt"* and carries the idea of cutting. May our words always be used to build others up and never to cut them down.

On the cross, while being tortured and mocked, Jesus could have yelled out curses to his killers, but he didn't; he offered up a prayer for them, setting the example for us. So, let's get rid of all bitterness, rage, anger, harsh words, and slander, as well as all types of evil behaviour. (Ephesians 4:31)

> *"Father, please give me the strength to control my anger. I want to release my anger to you, and I want to learn to respond to others who may hurt me with compassion and sensitivity, Amen."*

ARE YOU SPIRITUALLY ALIVE?

Read: Colossians 2:13-15

I once heard of an artist commissioned to paint a picture of a dying church. He imagined a decaying, abandoned building, a sanctuary empty and silent. But when he presented his masterpiece, the church leaders were shocked. His painting showed a large crowd of well-dressed people entering a church. Inside, the sanctuary gleamed with polished furnishings, youth were gathering in the foyer, and tables in the fellowship hall were filled with food and laughter. Everything appeared vibrant and full of life.

The artist explained his vision by turning to Scripture. He read the words of Jesus to the church in Sardis: *"Write this letter to the angel of the church in Sardis. This is the message from the one who holds the seven spirits of God and the seven stars. I know all the things you do; you have a reputation of being alive, but you are dead."* (Revelation 3:1 NIV)

He reminded them—and us—that a church can appear alive

outwardly, busy with activity, yet be spiritually dead inside. The same is true for individuals. We can go through the motions of faith, participate in church programs, and maintain a religious reputation—but what matters is whether we are spiritually alive in Christ.

Being spiritually alive begins with forgiveness. (Colossians 2:13 NIV) tells us, *"When you were dead in your sins and in the uncircumcision of your flesh, God made you alive with Christ. He forgave us all our sins."* Sin is a poison that infects every part of our being. Forgiveness is the medicine, the healing ointment, and the prescription that restores life. The moment our sins are forgiven, we are made new in Christ. As Paul reminds us in (2 Corinthians 5:17 NIV), *"Therefore, if anyone is in Christ, the new creation has come: The old has gone, the new is here!"* Forgiveness strips away the malice, bitterness, and selfishness of our old life and replaces it with gratitude, thankfulness, peace, and a desire to live for God.

Forgiveness also cancels our sins. (Colossians 2:14 NIV) says, *"Having canceled the charge of our legal indebtedness, which stood against us and condemned us; he has taken it away, nailing it to the cross."* This cancellation is total, which means that our past, present, and future sins are erased. God no longer holds them against us. (Jeremiah 31:34 NIV) assures us, *"For I will forgive their wickedness and will remember their sins no more."* This is why we can rejoice, knowing that the penalty for our sins has been removed. We are pardoned, free to worship and live with the joy of a clean slate.

This freedom is possible because our sins were nailed to the cross. When Christ went to the cross, He bore the full weight of our sin and broke its power over our lives. (Isaiah 53:5 NIV) declares, *"But he was pierced for our transgressions, he was crushed for our iniquities; the punishment that brought us peace was on him, and by his wounds we are healed."* Victory over sin is not just theological—it's practical. It allows us to live in the reality of God's grace, to walk each day in the newness of life, and to experience spiritual vitality.

Ask yourself: Is my life full of joy because my sins are forgiven? Have I truly claimed the victory of the cross? Spiritual life is not about appearances, busyness, or even reputation—it's about being alive in Christ. When Jesus returns, He wants to find us truly alive in Him, not just going through the motions.

Perhaps you feel spiritually dead because you have not yet committed your life to Christ. If that is your situation, there is hope. Confess your sins to God, thank Him for bearing the punishment of your sins on the cross, repent, and be baptized. When the Spirit convicts and people turn to Christ, they experience true spiritual life and walk in the freedom and joy that only Christ offers.

75

> *"Lord Jesus, thank You for Your sacrifice on the cross. Thank You for forgiving my sins, canceling the debt I could never repay, and making me alive in You. By the power of Your Holy Spirit, help me to live each day spiritually awake, joyful, and fruitful for Your glory. In Christ's name I pray, Amen."*

OVERCOMING OPPOSITION

Read: Nehemiah 4:1-8

In the late 1700s, the father of modern missions, William Carey, famously said, "Expect great things from God. Attempt great things for God." That statement still rings true today. Yet, like Nehemiah centuries before him, Carey understood an important reality: whenever we attempt great things for God, opposition is right around the corner. Spiritual progress almost always invites resistance.

As we turn to Nehemiah 4, we see that God's work often draws opposition from outside. Nehemiah faced hostility from Sanballat the Samaritan and his associates, who became furious when they heard the walls of Jerusalem were being rebuilt. Scripture tells us, *"They mocked and ridiculed the Jews… saying, 'What does this bunch of feeble Jews think they're doing?'"* (Nehemiah 4:2 NLT) Their anger was not merely personal—it was political and spiritual. A fortified Jerusalem threatened their control and influence in the region.

Opposition, however, is not a sign that God is absent. In many cases, it's evidence that God is at work. Charles Spurgeon once wisely said, "*God had one Son without sin, but He never had a son without trial.*" When God's people move forward in obedience, resistance often follows close behind. Yet opposition also presents an opportunity to foster a deeper dependence on God and renewed commitment to His purposes.

Interestingly, the outside pressure brought out the best in Nehemiah and the people. Instead of retreating, they rallied together. Nehemiah 4:6 tells us, "*At last the wall was completed... for the people had worked with enthusiasm*" (NLT). The ridicule did not weaken them—it strengthened their resolve. A shared sense of purpose united the people, reminding us that opposition can sometimes sharpen our focus and strengthen our faith.

But opposition does not always come from the outside. As we move into the next chapter, we discover that God's work can also face opposition from within. Nehemiah 5:1 says, "*About this time some of the men and their wives raised a cry of protest against their fellow Jews.*" Internal conflict, discouragement, and division can be just as threatening as external enemies.

When the enemy feels threatened by the advance of God's kingdom, he will use any means available. If he cannot stop the work from outside the walls, he will attempt to disrupt it from within. We see this pattern throughout Scripture. Jesus was mocked by the Pharisees—outsiders to His inner circle—and when that failed, Satan used Judas, one of the Twelve. Division within God's people has always been one of the enemy's most effective strategies.

Yet despite opposition, God's work will be accomplished. Nehemiah 6 records a triumphant conclusion: "*So on October 2 the wall was finished—just fifty-two days after we had begun. When our enemies... heard about it, they were frightened and humiliated. They realized this work had been done with the help of our God*" (Nehemiah 6:15–16 NLT). Whatever God begins, He will faithfully complete.

Still, we must remain alert. Even after defeat, Satan does not abandon the battlefield. Luke 4:13 reminds us that after tempting Jesus, "*The devil went away, waiting for another opportunity.*" Our enemy may retreat for a season, but he is always looking for a moment of weakness.

Satan seeks to use opposition as a weapon to discourage and derail us, but God can transform those same challenges into tools for growth and perseverance. Nehemiah's response offers timeless wisdom: *"But we prayed to our God and guarded the city day and night to protect ourselves"* (Nehemiah 4:9 NLT). Prayer, dependence on God, and faithful action will always be our best defence.

When opposition comes, may we respond as Nehemiah did: prayerful, watchful, united, and determined to finish the work God has placed before us.

> *"Lord, when opposition rises against the work You have called me to do, help me not to be discouraged or distracted. Teach me to pray first, to stay vigilant, and to trust fully in Your power. Strengthen my heart when criticism comes, guard my spirit from division, and help me remain faithful until the work You have begun in me is complete. In Jesus' name I pray, Amen."*

FIVE CHARACTERISTICS OF A PURE HEART

Read: 2 Timothy 2:22-26

Jesus said, "Blessed are the pure in heart, for they will see God" (Matthew 5:8 NIV). Few statements could be more searching or more hopeful. Scripture consistently presents the heart as the core of who we are. It is the center of our thoughts, emotions, desires, and decisions. Proverbs tells us that everything we do flows from it (Prov. 4:23). Our attitudes, convictions, and actions are all shaped by the condition of our hearts. If our hearts are pure, our lives will reflect that purity.

In 2 Timothy 2:22–26, the apostle Paul gives Timothy practical instruction on cultivating a pure heart in a challenging spiritual environment. From this passage, we can identify five key characteristics that mark a heart that is pleasing to God.

The first characteristic is a clear warning to flee youthful lusts. Paul writes, "*Flee the evil desires of youth*" (v. 22). The word "*flee*" is strong and urgent. It is not a suggestion but a command. In the original Greek, the word conveys the idea of running away from danger without hesitation. Just as Joseph fled from Potiphar's wife, believers are called to take sin seriously enough to put distance between themselves and temptation.

"Youthful lusts" include more than just sexual temptation. They also involve pride, impatience, reckless ambition, selfishness, and the desire for recognition. These are impulses that can quietly corrupt the heart if left unchecked. A pure heart begins by recognizing danger and choosing escape rather than compromise.

The remaining four characteristics are positive pursuits. Paul does not simply tell us what to run from; he tells us what to run toward.

The second characteristic is to pursue righteousness. Paul says, *"Pursue righteousness"* (v. 22). To pursue means to chase after with determination and effort. Righteousness refers to living in a way that aligns with God's standards and reflects His character. A believer who is not actively pursuing righteousness will inevitably drift toward sin. Obedience, time in God's Word, and a daily submission to the Spirit are essential in shaping a heart that desires what is right.

Third, we are called to pursue faith. This faith is not merely belief, but faithfulness—steadfast trust in God that results in obedience. Jesus rebuked the Pharisees because while they appeared religious on the outside, they neglected faithfulness on the inside (Matt. 23:23). A pure heart values integrity, loyalty, and dependability before God and others.

The fourth characteristic is the call to pursue love. Paul is referring to agape love—the selfless, sacrificial love that seeks the good of others. This is the love demonstrated by Christ and produced by the Holy Spirit. Love guards the heart from bitterness and pride. A pure heart does not merely avoid wrongdoing; it actively seeks to reflect God's compassion and grace toward others.

The fifth characteristic is the pursuit of peace. Paul urges Timothy to pursue peace *"along with those who call on the Lord out of a pure heart"* (v. 22). Peace is more than the absence of conflict; it's a settled harmony rooted in our relationship with God. While peace may not always be possible in every situation, believers are called to do everything within their power to live at peace with others (Rom. 12:18). A pure heart resists unnecessary quarrels and seeks unity within the body of Christ.

Paul reminds Timothy that even mature believers must remain vigilant. The Ephesian church was spiritually strong, yet Paul warned that opposition and spiritual traps remained. Satan continually looks for opportunities to ensnare God's servants (v. 26). Therefore, humility, gentleness, and dependence on God are essential in maintaining a pure heart.

A pure heart does not happen accidentally. It's formed through intentional choices. We need to choose every day to flee from sin, pursue godliness, and walk daily in the Spirit.

> *"Lord, my deepest desire is to have a heart that is pure before You. By the power of Your Holy Spirit, help me to flee from sinful desires and to pursue righteousness, faith, love, and peace. Guard my heart when temptation comes, keep me humble and teachable, and help my life reflect Your character. In my Savior's name, Amen."*

THE IMPORTANCE OF BAPTISM

Read: Romans 6:1-11

A buffet offers endless options, allowing people to pick and choose what suits their tastes. Unfortunately, some Christians approach God's commands the same way—selecting what feels comfortable while ignoring what feels inconvenient. Baptism is one command that is often treated this way. As a pastor, I have encountered many people who claimed to be Christians for years, yet had never been baptized. This reveals two serious concerns. First, they missed out on the blessing God attaches to obedience. Second, they were living in disobedience to a clear command of Christ.

Baptism is not a suggestion or a spiritual extra—it's an act of obedience. Jesus Himself made this unmistakably clear. In what we call the Great Commission, Jesus said, *"Therefore, go and make disciples of all the nations, baptizing them in the name of the Father and the Son and the Holy Spirit. Teach these new disciples to obey all the commands I have given you"* (Matthew 28:19–20 NLT). Baptism was never presented as optional or something to be postponed indefinitely. It was meant to be an immediate response to a genuine faith in Christ.

Scripture consistently teaches that baptism follows salvation. The Holman Concise Bible Dictionary explains it this way: *"Baptism comes after conviction of sin, repentance of sin, and confession of Christ as Lord and Savior. To be baptized is to preach a personal testimony through the symbol of baptism."* Baptism does not save us, but it publicly declares that we have been saved. In other words, it is an outward expression of an inward transformation.

In Romans 6:1–11, Paul explains the spiritual meaning behind baptism. He writes, *"For we died and were buried with Christ by baptism. And just as Christ was raised from the dead... now we also may live new lives"* (Romans 6:4 NLT). Full immersion baptism beautifully portrays the gospel. Going under the water represents death to our old way of life—our sin, our self-rule, and our former identity. Coming up out of the water pictures resurrection and a new life in Christ, empowered by His Spirit.

Baptism also reminds believers of their union with Christ. Paul continues, *"Since we have been united with him in his death, we will also be raised to life as he was"* (Romans 6:5 NLT). Baptism declares that our old self is no longer in control. Sin no longer reigns as our master because we now belong to Jesus. This truth is not only symbolic—it is transformational when embraced by faith.

Another important truth believers need to understand is that baptism brings blessings. God always honours obedience. One blessing is the joy and confidence that comes from knowing we are walking in God's will. Many believers who delay baptism struggle with a lack of assurance or spiritual stagnation, unaware they are withholding obedience in an area God has clearly addressed. Obedience opens the door for spiritual growth and deeper fellowship with the Lord.

There is also a communal blessing connected to baptism. When someone is baptized, their family, friends, and church family are encouraged and strengthened. Baptism serves as a public testimony of God's saving power and reminds all who witness it of their own commitment to Christ. It is a powerful moment of celebration and worship within the body of Christ.

To summarize this important command:
- Baptism in the New Testament was by full immersion.
- Baptism is for believers—those who have personally trusted Christ.
- Baptism symbolizes our death to sin and resurrection to new life in Christ.
- Baptism expresses our union, allegiance, and commitment to Jesus.

If you consider yourself a Christian but have not yet been baptized, you are missing out on a significant step of obedience and blessing. Scripture urges believers not to delay. Contact your pastor, take this step of faith, and publicly declare that Jesus Christ is your Lord and Saviour.

If you have already been baptized and you know someone who proclaims Christ as their Lord and Saviour but has yet to be baptized, please share this devotion with them and encourage them to take this step of obedience.

"Lord Jesus, thank You for the gift of salvation and for calling me to follow You in obedience. Help me never to treat Your commands lightly or selectively. Give me a heart that gladly obeys, trusting that Your ways are best. May baptism always be honoured, taught, and practiced as a joyful testimony of new life in Christ. In Jesus' name I pray, Amen."

GOD'S PERFECT PLAN

Read: Jeremiah 29:10-14

While driving one day, I noticed a turtle slowly making its way across a busy road. Concerned, I turned my car around to pick it up and carry it to safety. But by the time I reached the spot, the turtle was gone. As I continued on my way, that moment stayed with me. Later that day, the Lord brought a deeper realization to my heart: I, too, had once traveled down a road that led to certain spiritual death. Yet God, in His mercy, intervened. He took the time to save me and lead me beside still waters. That week, I bought a small stuffed turtle that still sits in my car window as a reminder of God's saving grace and perfect timing.

Today we will reflect on God's perfect plan—a plan that is always rooted in His goodness and faithfulness. Through the prophet Jeremiah, God spoke these comforting words to His people: "*For I know the plans I have for you… They are plans for good and not for disaster, to give you a future and a hope*" (Jeremiah 29:11 NLT). These words were not spoken in a season of ease but during a time of deep uncertainty and hardship.

God's plan first involves perseverance. In Jeremiah's day, God's people were facing seventy years of captivity in Babylon. This was not what they wanted. During their captivity, false prophets promised quick deliverance, but God warned His people not to listen to them. Instead, He called them to endure and to trust Him even when the path ahead was long and difficult.

When God asks us to walk through difficult seasons, our response must be trust. Scripture reminds us, *"Trust in the Lord with all your heart; do not depend on your own understanding. Seek his will in all you do, and he will show you which path to take"* (Proverbs 3:5–6 NLT). Perseverance grows when we stop leaning on our limited perspective and fully rely on God's wisdom and direction.

Secondly, the Lord's perfect plan involves prayer. In Jeremiah 29:12–13, God says, *"In those days when you pray, I will listen. If you look for me wholeheartedly, you will find me."* Prayer is not an emergency measure or a last resort—it's an essential part of walking in the Spirit. As one unknown writer noted, *"Prayer is not merely a defensive tool in times of crisis but a powerful offence against fear, doubt, and despair." (Unknown)*

Throughout Scripture, God promises to respond when His people humble themselves and seek Him. *"If my people… humble themselves and pray… I will hear from heaven"* (2 Chronicles 7:14 NLT). James also reminds us that *"The earnest prayer of a righteous person has great power and produces wonderful results"* (James 5:16, NLT). Prayer keeps our hearts aligned with God's purposes and reminds us that we are never facing our challenges alone.

Finally, God's plan requires patience. Seventy years of captivity meant that many of God's people would never see their return to Jerusalem in their lifetime. Yet God still called them to wait, trust, and believe that His promises would be fulfilled. Patience does not mean passivity. While waiting, God instructed them to build homes, plant gardens, marry, raise families, and seek the peace of the city where they lived (Jeremiah 29:5–7). In other words, they were to live faithfully and fruitfully right where God had planted them.

To wait on the Lord is to actively pursue Him. The word *"seek"* in Jeremiah 29:13 implies intentional pursuit. God's people were called to chase after Him with their whole hearts, even in a place where they did not want to be. God assured them that patience would eventually lead to restoration and blessing.

When we face seasons of uncertainty or disappointment, God invites us to persevere and patiently trust Him. "*The Lord is good to those who depend on him, to those who search for him*" (Lamentations 3:25, NLT). Let us never forget that His timing is always perfect, and His purposes will never fail.

> *"Heavenly Father, I desire for Your perfect plan to be fulfilled in my life. Teach me to persevere when the road is hard. I want to pray before I panic, and be patient as I wait on You. I want my plans to align with your perfect plan for me. So, today I place my future and my hope in Your faithful hands, Amen."*

If We Love Him...

Read: Jn 21:15-17; Pr 22:6; Mk 10:13-16

In May 2018, I attended a Pastors' Conference at the Moody Bible Institute in Chicago. It was a time of learning, reflection, and—most importantly—conviction. When I returned home, I stood before my congregation and asked for forgiveness. I confessed that I had let God, the church, my wife, my children, the church's children, and their parents down. I acknowledged that I had drifted from my calling, but I also committed to getting back on track with God's help.

Ephesians 4 teaches that the role of a pastor is to pray, preach, and equip the saints for the work of ministry. Somewhere along the way, I had lost that focus. I was attempting to minister in my own strength rather than depending on the Lord. That Sunday morning, I preached from a place of personal conviction, sharing what God had impressed upon my heart.

I began by reminding the church that if we love Him, we will feed

His lambs. In John 21:15–17, Jesus asked Peter three times, "*Do you love Me?*" Each time Peter answered yes, Jesus responded not with affirmation alone, but with instruction: "*Feed My lambs… Tend My sheep… Feed My sheep.*" Often, we focus on the question, but Jesus emphasized the response. Love for Christ is proven through obedient action.

The lambs Jesus referred to are the young and vulnerable—God's children. As a pastor and spiritual leader, I was responsible for helping feed and care for them with the truth of God's Word. Feeding the lambs is not about entertainment or activity alone; it's about intentional discipleship and spiritual nourishment.

At the conference, I attended a session titled "*Equipping or Entertaining.*" One statement that deeply affected me was this: "*Most research reveals that at least 50% of evangelical teenagers leave the church between the ages of 18 and 21, and few return. When one leaves, it's too many.*" That reality should burden every pastor, parent, and church leader. The goal of ministry is not to keep children busy, but to anchor them in a lasting faith.

Next, I shared that if we love Him, we will train our children in the way they should go. Proverbs 22:6 says, "*Train up a child in the way he should go, and when he is old he will not depart from it.*" This responsibility primarily belongs to parents, not the church alone. Pastors and church leaders are called to support and equip parents, but discipleship begins in the home.

"*The way*" spoken of in this verse has historically been understood as the faith—a life shaped by God's truth, values, and commands. Unfortunately, many parents expect the church to disciple their children while spiritual training at home is neglected. This was never God's design. The church should come alongside parents, not replace them.

During my message, I shared two additional statements that should cause all of us to pause and pray. One speaker said, "*We've spiced up the programs and ministries, but the wheat is not growing.*" Another said, "*It's time to admit that the current youth ministry model isn't aligned with a biblical framework.*" Programs alone cannot produce spiritual maturity. Only faithful teaching, godly example, and intentional discipleship can.

Finally, I reminded the church that if we love Him, we will bring our children to Jesus. In Mark 10:13–16, parents brought their children to Jesus. When the disciples rebuked them, Jesus responded firmly: "*Let the little children come to Me, and do not forbid them; for of such is the king-*

dom of God." Jesus welcomed children and blessed them, demonstrating His deep concern for young hearts and souls.

Christian parents, pastors, and church leaders must share this burden. If parents feel unqualified to disciple their children, church leaders should disciple the parents so they, in turn, can disciple their children. This is how we faithfully feed His lambs—by training them in the way they should go and bringing them to Jesus daily through prayer, teaching, and example. The truth is, if we truly love Him, our love will be seen in how we care for the next generation.

> *"Lord, You have entrusted us with the sacred responsibility of raising children in the faith. Forgive us where we have neglected or misunderstood our role. Help me to faithfully do my part so that the next generation will grow up knowing You, loving You, and walking in the Spirit. May we feed Your lambs with care and obedience, for Your glory. In Jesus' name I pray, Amen."*

ONE STEP AT A TIME

When Neil Armstrong stepped onto the surface of the moon in 1969, he famously said, "That's one small step for man, one giant leap for mankind." History often turns on a single step of courage. In a much quieter but far more significant way, our spiritual lives are also shaped by small, faith-filled steps taken in obedience to God.

The old hymn *"One Day at a Time, Sweet Jesus"* captures this truth beautifully: *"Just give me the strength to do every day what I have to do."* Following Jesus is not usually about giant leaps of faith, but about daily trust—sometimes even moment-by-moment dependence. Jesus Himself said that He came so we might have life and have it abundantly (John 10:10). That abundant life is experienced not all at once, but one step at a time.

In Matthew 14, we are invited to walk alongside Peter as he steps out of the boat in the middle of a violent storm. His experience teaches us powerful lessons about courage, obedience, and perseverance.

The first step Peter took was a courageous one. The disciples were in a boat late at night, battling strong winds and high waves. Suddenly, they saw a figure walking toward them on the water, and Scripture tells us they were terrified. But Jesus immediately spoke to them: *"Don't be afraid. Take courage. I am here!"* (Matthew 14:27 NLT) The phrase *"I am here"* echoes God's divine self-revelation. Jesus was reminding them that the One standing before them was not merely a teacher or a miracle-worker, but the living God in their midst.

In our own storms—whether emotional, spiritual, or circumstantial—we can take courage knowing that Jesus is present. He is not distant or unaware. He is the Master of the storm, and often He uses the storm itself to strengthen and refine our faith.

Courage, however, must be followed by obedience. Peter responded to Jesus by saying, *"Lord, if it's really you, tell me to come to you, walking on the water."* Jesus simply replied, *"Yes, come"* (Matthew 14:28–29 NLT). And Peter stepped out of the boat.

This moment is remarkable. Peter did not walk on water because he had a special ability, but because he trusted Jesus enough to obey His word. Obedience often requires us to leave what feels safe and familiar. Like Peter, we may struggle because obedience calls us to walk by faith, not by sight. Paul reminds us, *"We live by believing and not by seeing"* (2 Corinthians 5:7 NLT). The boat may feel secure, but obedience is where faith truly grows.

Peter walked toward Jesus, but then something changed: Peter's perseverance. Matthew tells us, *"But when he saw the strong wind and the waves, he was terrified and began to sink"* (v. 30). Peter did not fail because he stepped out; he faltered because he shifted his focus. When his eyes moved from Jesus to the storm, fear replaced faith.

Peter did not walk on water by his own strength either. He walked by faith. Perseverance means continuing to trust Jesus even when the storm rages, and fear whispers doubt in our ears. If we are going to be successful in maintaining our footing, we must persevere so we too don't waiver, stumble, and sink. James tells us to consider it joy when we face trials, because the testing of our faith develops perseverance. That perseverance must finish its work so we may become mature and complete. (Ja 1:2-4)

So, if you want to be mature and complete, living an abundant

Spirit-led life full of joy, you need to step out in courage, walk in obedience, and persevere in your faith.

> *"Lord Jesus, thank You for calling me to walk with You one step at a time. When storms arise, and fear begins to take hold, help me to fix my eyes on You and not on the waves around me. Give me the courage to step out in faith, the obedience to follow Your voice, and the perseverance to keep trusting You when the journey is difficult. In Your name I pray, Amen."*

Life is a Dash

Read: Job 7:7-9, 9:25-26, 14:1-2

Every headstone in a cemetery has two dates engraved on it—the date of birth and the date of death. Between those two dates is a small dash. That simple mark represents an entire life: every joy and sorrow, every success and failure, every decision and relationship. The dash may be small, but it tells a powerful story.

The psalmist prayed, "*Teach us to realize the brevity of life, so that we may grow in wisdom*" (Psalm 90:12, NLT). Scripture repeatedly reminds us that our time on earth is short, and God calls us to live wisely and faithfully with the days He gives us. Today, we will look at four images God uses in His Word to describe how brief our lives really are.

First, Scripture compares our life to a vapour. James writes, "*What is your life? You are a mist that appears for a little while and then disappears*" (James 4:14, NLT). A vapour or mist is visible for only a moment, easily dissolved by the rising sun. It reminds us how fragile and temporary life is. No matter how full our schedules can get or how long our plans extend into the future, none of us is guaranteed tomorrow. This truth is not meant to frighten us, but to awaken us and to remind us to live every day with gratitude and purpose.

Second, our life is compared to a breath. Job cries out, *"Remember that my life is but a breath, and I will never again feel happiness"* (Job 7:7, NLT). Take a deep breath in and then let it out. That brief moment, compared to eternity, illustrates how short our earthly life really is. We spend so much of our time holding tightly to the things that will not last—possessions, positions, and personal ambitions. Yet, Scripture urges us to loosen our grip and trust the eternal God who holds our future.

Third, the Bible compares our life to a cloud. Job says, *"As a cloud fades away and vanishes, so those who go down to the grave will never return"* (Job 7:9, NLT). Clouds drift across the sky, shaped by forces beyond their control, and they eventually disappear. We cannot stop them, slow them down, or make them stay. In the same way, life moves forward whether we are ready or not. This image reminds us that our time is not ours to command—it is entrusted to us by God.

Finally, Scripture compares our life to a flower. Peter writes, *"Our lives are like grass, and our beauty is like a flower in the field. The grass withers and the flower fades"* (1 Peter 1:24, NLT). Some flowers bloom for years; others, like the Queen of the Night, bloom for only a single evening, releasing a beautiful fragrance before withering by morning. Some lives seem tragically short—cut down while still in bloom. Yet Scripture assures us that God, the Master Gardener, knows exactly what He is doing. *"Precious in the sight of the Lord is the death of his faithful servants"* (Psalm 116:15, NLT). Our lives are never wasted in His hands.

Knowing how short life is should change how we live. Sadly, many people live selfishly, as though they will never die. The psalmist observed that wise and foolish alike pass away, leaving their wealth behind, even though many live as if their legacy will last forever (Psalm 49:10–12). Titles fade, possessions are redistributed, and accomplishments will soon be forgotten after you and me are gone—but our faithfulness to God will endure forever.

That is why Scripture urges believers to *"make the most of every opportunity in these evil days"* (Ephesians 5:16, NLT). To redeem time means to value it, invest it wisely, and rescue it from being wasted. Our time is limited here on earth, but our reward is eternal. Paul reminds us that there is laid up for believers *"a crown of righteousness"* for all who love and long for Christ's appearing (2 Timothy 4:8, NLT).

The dash on your headstone may be small, but it matters greatly. How you live today shapes the story it tells. May our lives not be lived out foolishly, but faithfully—so that when our dash is etched into our headstone, it will point others to the glory of God.

> *"Dear Lord, Your word has reminded me today that my life on this earth is brief and my days are numbered. Help me to live wisely with the time You have given me. Teach me to value what truly matters and to walk faithfully with You. I want to use my days for Your glory, and may the dash of my life tell a story of faith, hope, and love. In the name of Jesus, I pray, Amen."*

THE REDEEMER AND THE REDEEMED

Read: Ephesians 1:7-12

Everyone needs encouragement, and few passages in Scripture provide it as richly as Paul's letter to the church in Ephesus. Written not only to one congregation but circulated among the surrounding churches, this letter reminds believers who they are in Christ and what God has done on their behalf. As Paul reflects on redemption and inheritance, his words still encourage us today, pointing us to the Redeemer and those who have been redeemed.

Over the years, I have purchased vehicles and eventually traded them in. Even though they were no longer new, they still had value. Someone was willing to buy them back, restore them, and put them to good use again. In a far greater and more meaningful way, this simple illustration helps us understand what Paul is teaching about redemption. We had value to God—not because of our perfection, but because of His love—and He was willing to pay the price to redeem us.

Paul begins by drawing our attention to God's purchase. He writes, *"In him we have redemption through his blood, the forgiveness of sins, in accordance with the riches of God's grace that he lavished on us"* (Ephesians 1:7–8 NIV). Redemption means to buy back, and the cost of our freedom was nothing less than the blood of God's Son. This reminds us that our salvation was not cheap—it was costly, and motivated by grace.

God is the Redeemer. He redeems those who confess with their mouths that Jesus is Lord and believe in their hearts that God raised Him from the dead (Romans 10:9). Through Christ, we are forgiven, restored, and set free from the power and penalty of sin. We are no longer owned by our past failures or bound by guilt because we belong to God.

Paul also reminds us that redemption was always part of God's plan. He tells us that God *"made known to us the mystery of his will according to his good pleasure, which he purposed in Christ"* (Ephesians 1:9 NIV). God's plan was not an afterthought in response to human failure. Before the foundation of the world, He planned to bring salvation through Jesus Christ.

While we may not understand every detail of God's plan, we do know this: He invites us to participate in it. Through the Great Commission, God calls every believer to share the good news of redemption with others. God does not need us to accomplish His purposes, yet in His grace, He chooses to involve us. This truth gives our lives meaning and direction beyond ourselves.

Paul expands on this idea in another letter when he writes, *"For we are God's handiwork, created in Christ Jesus to do good works, which God prepared in advance for us to do"* (Ephesians 2:10 NIV). We are not saved by good works, but we are saved for them. Redemption leads to transformation, and transformation leads to a life that reflects God's grace and glory.

Not only has God purchased us and revealed His plan to us, but He has also given us a priceless inheritance. Paul writes, *"In him we were also chosen… in order that we… might be for the praise of his glory"* (Ephesians 1:11–12 NIV). This inheritance is not temporary or uncertain. It's eternal.

Matthew Henry described this inheritance beautifully when he wrote, *"The eternal inheritance is the great blessing with which we are blessed in Christ: Heaven is the inheritance, the happiness of which is a sufficient portion for a soul: it is conveyed in the way of an inheritance, being the gift of a Father to his children." (Matthew Henry Commentary)* This means that our inheritance is not merely a future reward; it is the hope that anchors us in the present. Knowing what awaits us gives us the strength to endure trials and the motivation to live faithfully.

Paul concludes this section by reminding us that everything God has done—our redemption, forgiveness, purpose, and inheritance—is meant to result in praise. Our lives should reflect gratitude for God's grace and faithfulness in sharing what He has done with others.

To summarize these encouraging truths:

- God has purchased our freedom through the blood of Christ.
- God has forgiven us according to the riches of His grace.
- God has revealed His eternal plan to us in Christ.
- God has promised us a priceless and eternal inheritance.

For these reasons, God alone is worthy of our praise.

"Lord Jesus, thank You for redeeming me at such a great cost. I am humbled knowing that You purchased my freedom and forgave my sins by Your grace. Thank You for revealing Your plan and inviting me to be part of Your work, and may all that I do bring glory to You, Amen."

DAY 34

CALLED TO SERVE

Read: Galatians 5:13-14

Imagine a family that finally pays off their mortgage. One child responds by creating a long list of new house rules—what rooms can be used, how late the lights must be on, who is allowed to visit—determined to protect the home by control. Another child responds by throwing out all boundaries altogether—late-night parties, no chores, no care for the property—believing ownership means freedom from responsibility. Both responses miss the point.

The house wasn't paid off so the family could live in fear of breaking rules or falling into neglect, but so they could enjoy it and care for it together. The conflict arises because each child misunderstands what freedom truly means.

That is exactly the conflict Paul addresses in the churches of Galatia. Some believers clung to rules and works, believing obedience earned God's favour. Others treated grace as permission to live however they pleased. Paul writes to remind them—and us—that freedom in Christ is neither bondage to rules nor abandonment of responsibility. It is freedom with purpose and a call to serve one another in love.

The two groups of people in Galatia Paul addressed were the legalists and their works theology and those who abused God's grace by adopting the attitude that they were set free from any moral or civil obligation. Paul wrote this letter to try to reconcile their differences. He was trying to tell them that those who are set free were not set free to sin; they have been set free to serve.

But sometimes we Christians serve for the wrong reasons, like guilt. Some new Christians who haven't fully grasped the teaching of God's grace may serve because they feel they need to make up for past wrongs.

Others may serve out of tradition. Some Christians serve in the church because their parents and grandparents did, and so on. However, if someone's service is driven by tradition rather than love, it is misguided.

Some serve to seek God's approval. This is a dangerous motivation because we cannot win or earn God's approval or acceptance. The work's theology teaches that if I do more, I'll be approved and accepted more, and with God, that is just not true or possible.

We must evaluate our motives for serving, because if our service is self-oriented rather than other-oriented, we will be out of balance.

If you want to serve with the right attitude and motives, ask God through prayer to show you how. A very famous US President once said, *"Ask not what your country can do for you; ask what you can do for your country." President John F. Kennedy*

Try personalizing this as a prayer. Try asking not what Christ can do for you, ask what you can do for Christ! Ask not what your church can do for you, ask what you can do for your church! Ask not what your spouse can do for you, ask what you can do for your spouse! And..Ask not what your neighbour can do for you, ask what you can do for your neighbour! God will guide you, and whatever you do, do it as though you were working for the Lord and not man. (Col 3:23)

Jesus served a lot of people. He didn't have to serve them. He did it because of his great love for mankind, and we should do the same.

Opportunities are plenty, and when you trust in the Lord with all your heart and allow him to direct your paths (Proverbs 3:5-6), he will make a way and a place of suitable service for you and for me.

> "Lord, thank You for the freedom I have in Christ. Help me to never abuse that freedom or take it for granted. Search my heart and purify my motives so that my service flows from love, not guilt or self-interest. Teach me to serve others the way Jesus did and guide me to the places You want me to serve. In Jesus' name I pray, Amen."

IN THE MASTER'S HANDS

Read: Matthew 14:15-22

Jesus performed many miracles during His earthly ministry, but the feeding of the five thousand stands out as especially significant. It is the only miracle—apart from the resurrection—recorded in all four Gospels. That alone tells us the Holy Spirit wants us to pay close attention. This miracle is rich with meaning and purpose, revealing not only who Jesus is, but also what He can do with what is placed in His hands.

First, this miracle illustrates Jesus Christ as the Bread of Life, who would one day be broken on the cross for the sins of humanity. Later in John's Gospel, Jesus makes this connection clear when He says, *"I am the bread of life. Whoever comes to me will never be hungry again"* (John 6:35 NLT). The bread multiplied that day pointed forward to His body, which would be given as a sacrifice for all mankind.

Second, this miracle showed the Jewish people that One greater than Moses had arrived. Many Jews believed Moses had given their ancestors bread in the wilderness, but Jesus corrected that misunderstanding: "*Moses didn't give you bread from heaven. My Father did. And now he offers you the true bread from heaven*" (John 6:32–33 NLT). Jesus was declaring Himself to be the true provision of God—greater than manna, greater than Moses, and greater than anything the world could offer.

Third, this miracle demonstrated Jesus' power as Lord over all creation. With a simple prayer and obedient hands, He multiplied a small offering into an abundant provision. Nothing is impossible when it rests in the Master's hands.

With that in mind, let's look more closely at what Jesus did with the bread and consider what it means for us to place our lives in His hands.

The Master Blessed the Bread

Matthew tells us that Jesus took the loaves, looked up toward heaven, and gave thanks (v. 19). Before the bread was multiplied, it was blessed. Jesus acknowledged the Father as the source of all provision. Giving thanks was a regular practice for both Jesus and the Jewish people. The apostle Paul reminds us that, "*Everything God created is good, and we should not reject any of it but receive it with thanks*" (1 Timothy 4:4 NLT).

This reminds us that God desires to bless those who willingly place themselves in His hands. Gratitude positions our hearts to receive His blessing. When we acknowledge Him as our provider, we open ourselves to His work in our lives.

The Master Broke the Bread

After blessing the bread, Jesus broke it. The same hands that blessed were the hands that broke. This can be difficult for us to accept. We enjoy God's blessings, but we often resist His breaking. Yet Scripture shows us that brokenness often precedes usefulness.

God allowed Job—a righteous and faithful man—to experience deep loss before expanding his influence and blessing him even more greatly (see Job 1:1–3). Brokenness humbles us, removes our self-reliance, and teaches us to depend fully on God. Sometimes the Lord must break us so that what He has placed within us can be shared with others.

The Master Broadened the Bread

Finally, Jesus broadened—or multiplied—the bread. Five small loaves and two fish were insignificant in human terms. They could barely feed one boy, yet in the Master's hands, they became enough to feed between ten and fifteen thousand people, with leftovers to spare.

This is what God does with what we offer Him. He doesn't ask for abundance—He asks for availability. When we surrender what little we have, He has the power to broaden it beyond anything we could imagine.

As you reflect on this miracle, can you remember the blessings you've received since placing yourself in the Master's hands? Are you willing to trust Him not only with blessing, but also with breaking—so that He might use you to broaden His work through you? I pray that you will.

> *"Lord, today I place my life once again into Your hands. Thank You for every blessing You have given me, even when I didn't recognize it at the time. Help me to trust You during seasons of breaking, knowing that You are shaping me for Your purposes, and may my life be a testimony of what You can do with a willing heart. I am Yours, Amen."*

A CALL TO WORSHIP

Read: Romans 12:1-8

You may be familiar with the story of Cain and Abel—two brothers who each brought an offering to the Lord. Abel's offering was accepted, but Cain's was rejected. Scripture tells us that Cain became angry and discouraged. God lovingly warned him, saying, "Why are you angry? … If you do what is right, will you not be accepted? But if you do not do what is right, sin is crouching at your door; it desires to have you, but you must rule over it" (Genesis 4:6–7 NIV).

Cain ignored God's warning. His heart hardened, jealousy took root, and eventually, he murdered his brother. All of this stemmed from an act of worship that was not offered with the right heart. This sobering account reminds us that worship is not just about what we bring to God, but how and why we bring it.

Many people think worship begins and ends with singing. While singing is certainly a beautiful expression of worship, Scripture teaches us that worship encompasses everything we do for God. Our giving, our service, our obedience, and even the way we live our daily lives are all acts of worship. In Romans 12:1–2, the apostle Paul outlines what acceptable worship truly looks like, calling believers to a transformed, surrendered life.

Worship Begins with Sacrificing Your Body

Paul opens with a heartfelt appeal: "*And so, dear brothers and sisters, I plead with you to give your bodies to God because of all he has done for you*" (Romans 12:1a NLT). The word "*plead*" (or "*beseech*" in the NKJV) conveys the idea of urgent begging or earnest urging. Paul is calling believers to respond to God's mercy with total surrender.

He continues, "*Let them be a living and holy sacrifice—the kind he will find acceptable. This is truly the way to worship him*" (Romans 12:1b NLT). Unlike Old Testament sacrifices that were dead on the altar, we are called to be living sacrifices—daily offering our bodies, actions, and behaviours to God. Paul reminds us why this matters: "*For you were bought at a price; therefore glorify God in your body and in your spirit, which are God's*" (1 Corinthians 6:20 NKJV).

Worship Continues by Submitting Your Mind

Paul then turns to the mind: "*Do not conform to the pattern of this world, but be transformed by the renewing of your mind*" (Romans 12:2a NIV). The world constantly pressures us to think, speak, and act in ways that oppose God's truth. God's desire, however, is transformation from the inside out.

The word "*transformed*" comes from the Greek **metamorphoō**, which gives us the word metamorphosis. It describes a complete inner change that results in an outward difference. This transformation happens as we renew our minds through God's Word. Paul exhorts Timothy—and us—to "*work hard so you can present yourself to God and receive his approval... correctly explaining the word of truth*" (2 Timothy 2:15 NLT). A renewed mind leads to discerning choices and Christlike living.

Worship Is Completed by Surrendering Your Will

Finally, Paul speaks of yielding our will to God: "*Then you will be able to test and approve what God's will is—his good, pleasing and perfect will*" (Romans 12:2b NIV). When God has our bodies and our minds, He also desires our wills.

Jesus modelled this perfectly in the Garden of Gethsemane when He prayed, "*Father, if it is Your will, take this cup away from Me; nevertheless not My will, but Yours, be done*" (Luke 22:42 NKJV). Like Jesus, we are called to regularly spend time alone with God—yielding our desires, plans, and ambitions to Him.

When we live this way, worship becomes a lifestyle. Paul reminds us, "*Whatever you do, do it heartily, as to the Lord and not to men*" (Colossians 3:23 NKJV). Every act, no matter how small, can become sacred when done for God's glory.

> *"Lord, I come before You today with a grateful heart, offering You my body as a living sacrifice—holy and acceptable in Your sight. I willingly surrender my will to Yours, trusting that Your plans are good, pleasing, and perfect. May my life be an act of worship that honours You in all things. In Jesus' name I pray, Amen."*

THE POWER OF ENCOURAGEMENT (PART ONE)

Read: Hebrews 10:24-25

On June 18, 1956, a tragic and heroic accident occurred on Schroon Lake in New York. A speeding motorboat hit a wave and violently threw two passengers into the water—a fifty-year-old man and a little girl. The little girl could not swim. Realizing the danger she was in, the man immediately held her head above the water while the boat circled back. The girl was rescued, but the man, exhausted and unable to keep himself afloat, sank beneath the water and drowned.

That man was Dawson Trotman, the founder of The Navigators, an international discipleship ministry that continues to impact lives worldwide. Shortly after his death, Time Magazine reported these words: *"He lived to save others. His death was just the way he would have planned it."*

Reverend Billy Graham preached at Dawson Trotman's funeral and said simply yet powerfully, *"Dawson Trotman was always lifting someone up."* His life stands as a lasting testimony to the power of encouragement. When all is said and done, I hope that when your life is remembered—and when mine is remembered—people will say that we were individuals who consistently lifted others up.

As we turn to our passage today, Hebrews 10:24–25, we are introduced to a vital biblical principle: encouragement. The writer says, "*Let us think of ways to motivate one another to acts of love and good works. And let us not neglect our meeting together, as some people do, but encourage one another, especially now that the day of his return is drawing near.*" (NLT)

In the Greek language, the word "*encourage*" means "*to call to one's side, to comfort, to console, and to strengthen.*" Encouragement is not passive; it's intentional and personal. It involves coming alongside someone and helping them stand firm when they might otherwise fall.

When the book of Hebrews was written, believers were facing intense persecution. Life was hard, and faith was costly. And in difficult times, our natural tendency is to protect ourselves and look inward. Yet, instead of urging self-preservation, this letter calls believers to look outward and to encourage one another. It's been said that, "*Encouragement is the kind of expression that helps someone want to be a better Christian, even when life is rough…To encourage is to inspire another with courage.*" *(Larry Crab and Dan Allender)* That captures the heart of this passage.

There is a beautiful connection in the original language that deepens this truth. The Greek word for "*encourage*" in Hebrews 10:25 is **parakaleo**. The Greek word used for the Comforter—the Holy Spirit—in John 14:16 is **parakletos.** Both come from the same root word. This suggests that when we genuinely encourage one another, we reflect the very ministry of the Holy Spirit. Encouragement becomes evidence that the Spirit of God truly dwells within us.

Another important detail is that the word encourage in this passage is written in the active voice. That means we do not wait for encouragement to come to us—we are to take the initiative. We are called to encourage others regularly and intentionally. Hebrews 3:12–13 reminds us to exhort one another daily so that no one becomes hardened by sin's deceitfulness. Encouragement is not optional; it's essential for spiritual survival.

It's also been said that, "*We live by encouragement and die without it — slowly, sadly and angrily.*" *(Celeste Holm)* How true is that? You see, our words and actions matter. A timely word of hope, gratitude, or affirmation can be the very thing that keeps someone standing when life feels overwhelming.

I'll leave you with this thought from William Barclay: "*It is easy to laugh at men's ideals; it is easy to discourage others. The world is full of discouragers. We have a Christian duty to encourage one another. Many a time a word of praise or thanks or appreciation or cheer has kept a man on his feet. Blessed is the man who speaks such a word.*" May we be those people—men and women who consistently lift others up. Who can you encourage and lift up today?

> *"Lord, thank You for the encouragement You continually give me through Your Word, Your Spirit, and Your people. Help me to notice those around me who are weary, discouraged, or struggling. Give me the courage and compassion to come alongside them with words and actions that build up rather than tear down, Amen."*

THE POWER OF ENCOURAGEMENT (PART TWO)

Read: Hebrews 11:22-25

As we revisit the power of encouragement, we now turn our attention to a person of encouragement—a flesh-and-blood example we can learn from and imitate. That person is Joseph. You may ask, which Joseph? Well, this Joseph is better known by his nickname: Barnabas. Scripture introduces him to us in Acts 4, and his life quickly reveals why encouragement became his defining characteristic.

Luke records these words about the early church: *"There were no needy people among them, because those who owned land or houses would sell them and bring the money to the apostles to give to those in need. For instance, there was Joseph, the one the apostles nicknamed Barnabas (which means 'Son of Encouragement'). He was from the tribe of Levi and came from the island of Cyprus. He sold a field he owned and brought the money to the apostles."* (Acts 4:34–37 NLT)

Joseph was given the nickname Barnabas—*"Son of Encourage-*

ment"—because of this unselfish and sacrificial act. He didn't seek recognition, position, or power. Instead, he quietly met a need. His encouragement was not merely spoken; it was demonstrated through generosity and obedience. Encouragement often begins with seeing a need and responding with compassion.

The apostles recognized something special in Barnabas. They put their seal of approval on him, and later Paul would describe him this way: *"Barnabas was a good man, full of the Holy Spirit and strong in faith."* (Acts 11:24 NLT)

That is a powerful description. Barnabas wasn't known for eloquent preaching or dramatic miracles. He was known for being good, Spirit-filled, and Spirit-Led—qualities that fuelled his ministry of encouragement.

One of the most significant examples of Barnabas' encouragement is found in his relationship with Saul, who would later become the apostle Paul. At that time, Saul had a terrifying reputation. He was known as a fierce persecutor of Christians. After his dramatic encounter with the Lord on the road to Damascus, Saul traveled to Jerusalem and attempted to join the disciples. Scripture tells us they were all afraid of him, doubting whether his conversion was genuine.

It was Barnabas who stepped in. *"Then Barnabas brought him to the apostles and told them how Saul had seen the Lord on the way to Damascus and how the Lord had spoken to Saul."* (Acts 9:27 NLT)

Barnabas took a risk. He believed in Saul when no one else would. He stood beside a man everyone else avoided. Without Barnabas' encouragement, Saul's ministry may have stalled before it ever began.

Later, when God opened a door of ministry in Antioch, Barnabas was sent to investigate. Scripture says, *"When he arrived and saw this evidence of God's blessing, he was filled with joy, and he encouraged the believers to stay true to the Lord."* (Acts 11:23 NLT) Barnabas didn't criticize or control. He encouraged, and then came the result? *"And many people were brought to the Lord."* (Acts 11:24 NLT)

Barnabas then did something remarkable—he went looking for Saul in Tarsus. Rather than feeling threatened by Saul's gifts, Barnabas brought him alongside himself. *"Barnabas went on to Tarsus to look for Saul. When he found him, he brought him back to Antioch. Both of them stayed there with the church for a full year, teaching large crowds of people."* (Acts 11:25–26 NLT)

Barnabas remained true to his nickname. His encouragement helped shape the ministry of the man who would later write thirteen New Testament letters. We owe a great deal to Barnabas because he saw potential where others saw fear.

Charles Swindoll once said, "*I know of no one more needed, more valuable, more Christ-like than the individual who is committed to the ministry of encouragement.*" That was Barnabas. And it can be us, too. Who can you encourage today? You may never know how God might use that simple act of faith.

> *"Lord Jesus, thank You for the example of Barnabas and for showing me the power of encouragement lived out in real life. Help me to see people the way You see them, not as they are now, but as they could become through Your grace. Bring someone into my path today whom I can encourage—through my words, my actions, or my generosity. In Your name I ask these things, Amen."*

Our Choices Make Us Who We Are

Read: Galatians 5:16-26

Poor choices — we've all made them. Some have left only minor scratches on our lives, while others have carved deep marks that take years to heal. Yet every decision shapes us in one way or another. The fact is that our choices—good or bad—make us who we are.

Anne Frank said, *"Our lives are fashioned by our choices. First, we make our choices. Then our choices make us."* She said that from a place of deep reflection, and even a fictional character like Spider-Man echoed the same truth when he said, *"It's our choices that make us who we are, and we can always make the right choices."* I can't believe I just quoted Spiderman in a Christian devotional. However, both point to an undeniable reality: life is built on choices, and every day we stand at a crossroads between the flesh and the Spirit.

In today's passage, Paul tells the Galatians they must make a choice, and the kind of fruit produced will either be good or bad. This is why we need to consider two important factors in making wise, Spirit-led choices.

First, Paul gives us the command to walk by the Spirit so that we will not gratify the desires of the flesh (v. 16). The Greek word for "*walk*" is **peripateo**, meaning "*to conduct one's life.*" It's written in the present tense, implying an ongoing, daily process — progress from where we are to where God wants us to be. Walking in the Spirit is not a one-time act but a continuous movement forward, step by step, choice by choice.

To walk in the Spirit means learning to "*let go and let God,*" *(Unknown)* which, as we all know, is easier said than done. It's letting go of self-reliance and learning to trust in God's truth, God's power, and God's Word every single day. It's choosing faith over fear, surrender over stubbornness, and obedience over impulse.

However, the desire to obey this command leads us directly into conflict (vv. 17–18) because God has given us free will. These verses make it clear: "*the Spirit*" and "*the flesh*" are in constant conflict with each other. This means the Spirit-led life is not easy—it's a constant battle. Paul understood this struggle deeply. He confessed, "*Nothing good dwells in me, that is, in my flesh*" (Romans 7:18 NKJV), and again, "*I practice the very evil that I do not wish, and the good I wish I do not do*" (Romans 7:19, NKJV). Even Jesus, in Gethsemane, told His disciples, "*The spirit is willing, but the flesh is weak*" (Matthew 26:41 NKJV).

Christian, you need to know or be reminded that your life is a battlefield. Every day, choices are arrows aimed at either victory or defeat. But take heart—victory is always possible. You can do all things through Christ who strengthens you (Philippians 4:13). No matter the struggle, difficulty, or temptation, Christ lives in you. His power indwells those who have received eternal life through faith in Him (John 17:2). That power is not distant—it's personal, present, and available every moment you choose to yield to the Spirit's leading.

The best way to "*make no provision for the flesh*" (Romans 13:14, NKJV) is to avoid the paths that lead you toward temptation and instead run toward the Spirit. Seek His counsel through prayer, Scripture, and godly community. Small, faithful decisions—one choice at a time, one day at a time, and sometimes one moment at a time will help develop the habit of walking daily in the Spirit of God.

So when the next choice comes—and it always will—pause and ask, which nature am I feeding? Because the fruit you bear tomorrow will be the result of the choices you make today.

"Lord, help me to walk in Your Spirit today. Give me wisdom to make the right choices, strength to resist temptation, and courage to follow Your leading. May the fruit of my life reflect Your presence in me, Amen".

DAY 40

TRANSFORMING TRUTH

Read: Ephesians 4:11-21

Marilyn Monroe was once asked if she adhered to a particular faith. Her response was telling: "I believe in everything—a little." That statement captures the mindset of many people today. Truth is treated like a buffet, where individuals select what feels right and leave the rest behind.

A Barna Group study taken some years ago revealed that only 22 percent of participants agreed with the statement, "*There are moral truths that are absolute, meaning those moral truths or principles do not change according to the circumstances.*" That means 78 percent did not believe in absolute moral truth. This raises an important question: do we really believe that truth is flexible, or do we simply apply that belief selectively?

In everyday life, most of us live as if absolute truth exists. When we flip on a light switch, we trust the reality of electricity. When we drive a car, we believe in the effectiveness of a combustion engine. We don't debate those truths or redefine them based on personal preference. We rely on them because they work. In the same way, Scripture teaches that there is an absolute spiritual truth—a truth that is real, reliable, and transforming.

If absolute truth exists, then it follows that there is also a transforming truth, and that truth is described for us in Ephesians 4. In verse 21, Paul makes a striking statement when he writes about *"the truth that is in Jesus."* It's important to note that this is the only place in the entire letter where Paul uses the name Jesus without attaching the title Lord or Christ. This is intentional.

Paul is making it clear that truth is not merely a concept or a philosophy—truth is a person. Jesus Himself said, *"I am the way and the truth and the life"* (John 14:6, NIV). Here, Paul echoes that same truth by pointing us to the sinless, spotless life that Jesus lived while He walked on this earth. The life of Jesus was the living demonstration of the truth that resided within Him.

Jesus is the person of truth, and only the person of truth has the power to truly transform a life. In Ephesians 4:11–19, Paul describes the condition of unbelievers—spiritually ignorant people, darkened in their understanding, and hardened in their hearts. They live without direction and without discernment. In contrast, those who are transformed by the person of truth are no longer *"infants, tossed back and forth by the waves, and blown here and there by every wind of teaching"* (v. 14).

Instead, Paul says, *"Speaking the truth in love, we will grow to become in every respect the mature body of him who is the head, that is, Christ"* (v. 15). Spiritual maturity comes from being anchored in the truth—not cultural truth and not personal truth, but the truth found in Jesus.

Transformation does not happen by accident. Verse 21 reminds us that transformation occurs *"when you heard about Christ and were taught in him in accordance with the truth that is in Jesus."* This is why pastors and teachers are essential to the life of the church. God uses them to faithfully teach the truth so that believers can grow, mature, and be equipped for service.

Jesus Himself emphasized this when He said, *"If you hold to my teaching, you are really my disciples. Then you will know the truth, and the truth will set you free"* (John 8:31–32 NIV). Truth brings freedom, but only when it is received and obeyed.

Attending church alone will not transform you. Fellowship by itself will not transform you. Learning about Christ without submitting to Him will not transform you. Even serving Christ with the wrong motives will not produce transformation. True change happens when we genuinely hear Jesus, respond to His teaching, and put it into practice with hearts surrendered to Him. That deserves repeating, with hearts surrendered to Him.

When we submit our will to the person of truth, His truth begins to reshape our thinking, values, relationships, and conduct. Over time, we are transformed into the people He desires us to be—not by our own effort, but by obedient faith in the One who truly transforms.

"Lord, I desire to be transformed into Your likeness. I want my life to reflect Your truth in a world that is confused and divided. Today, I surrender my will to Yours and ask You to teach me through Your Word, and may others see You living through me as I follow the person of truth—Jesus, Amen."

The Purpose of Praise

Read: Psalm 150:1-6

Have you ever been in a worship service so filled with the Spirit of God that you didn't want your time with Him to end? I experienced that while serving as a Chaplain with a Billy Graham Rapid Response International Team in Brussels, Belgium, just days after two suicide bombers killed thirty-two people and injured hundreds in March of 2016. One evening after praying on the streets with people at one of the makeshift memorials, our team met with local church leaders who were grieving, shaken, and searching for hope. As we gathered in prayer, something powerful happened. God completely took over our praise time, and the room was filled with the glory and the presence of the Lord. In the midst of tragedy, praise became a holy refuge.

Praise is often the catalyst that ushers us into God's presence. Yet praise is far more than singing a song or lifting our hands during a service. Psalm 150 shows us that praise is purposeful, intentional, and deeply spiritual.

First, praise is a lifestyle. It's easy to praise God when life is good—when prayers are answered, and circumstances are favourable. But what about when you feel sad, hurt, lonely, lost, discouraged, or disappointed? Praise becomes especially powerful when it's all you have left to give. In those moments, God promises to carry you. "*Listen to Me… I have made, and I will bear; even I will carry, and will deliver you*" (Isaiah 46:3–4, NKJV). Praise reminds us that we are never abandoned, even when life feels overwhelming.

There is also an important distinction between praise and worship. They are not the same, yet they cannot be separated. Praise is celebratory—it proclaims who God is and what He has done. Worship is intimate—it draws us close to the heart of God. When we praise the Lord, we are often led naturally into worship, where gratitude and love flow freely, whether in good times or bad. This brings glory to God and opens our hearts to experience His presence more deeply.

Psalm 150 answers several key questions about praise.

Where can we praise God? Everywhere and at any time. "*Praise God in His sanctuary; praise Him in His mighty firmament!*" (v.1).

Why do we praise God? "*For His mighty acts; praise Him according to His excellent greatness!*" (v.2).

How can we praise God? Verses 3–5 list a variety of instruments and expressions, reminding us that praise is creative, joyful, and expressive.

Who should praise the Lord? "*Let everything that has breath praise the Lord*" (v.6). Praise is for every living, breathing creature.

Praise also brings peace. It is God's remedy for the spirit of heaviness (Isaiah 61:3). When we praise God in the middle of the storm, our focus shifts from ourselves to Him, and His peace, "*which surpasses all understanding,*" guards our hearts and minds (Philippians 4:7).

Finally, praise is a weapon. Our praise defeats the enemy. It causes walls to fall, as in the days of Joshua. It silences the fury of fire, as with the Hebrew boys. It shuts the mouths of lions, as with Daniel. Praise declares that God is greater than our circumstances.

So, in the midst of your circumstances—whatever they are—praise Him. In the middle of confusion—praise Him. In the face of crisis—praise Him. And let everything that has breath praise the Lord.

"Lord, no matter what is happening in my life, I choose to praise You. Teach me to live a lifestyle of praise, not only when things are good, but especially when life is hard. May the sacrifice of my praise bring peace to my heart and glory to Your name, Amen."

AGEING WITH GRACE

Read: Ecclesiastes 12:1-8

As we grow older—Lord willing—the desire of God for our lives is that we would age with grace. Ageing is inevitable, I know, because this coming spring, in June of 2026, I will turn sixty years old. But how we age spiritually is shaped by the choices we make along the way. In today's passage from Ecclesiastes 12, Solomon offers wisdom to help us understand how to grow old well. From this text, we see at least three principles that guide us toward ageing with grace, beginning with the importance of a strong faith developed early in life.

Solomon begins with this exhortation: "*Remember your Creator in the days of your youth, before the days of trouble come and the years approach when you will say, 'I find no pleasure in them'*" (v.1). A life anchored in God from an early age builds a foundation that can withstand the challenges that inevitably come with time.

I did not become a follower of Christ until I was in my late thirties. While I am deeply grateful for God's grace in saving me when He did, I clearly see the blessing of those who have followed Christ from a young age. They have had the opportunity to walk with Him through every season of life—to know Him not only in hardship but also in strength, growth, and purpose. Remembering our Creator early shapes the direction of our entire lives. Please remember this as you see the younger generation in the church.

Sadly, many young people today feel they don't have time for God. They resist allowing Him to lay the foundation in their lives, choosing instead to live only for the moment. That reality makes it critically important for the seniors in our churches to play an active role in the spiritual upbringing of the next generation. God never intended faith to be lived in isolation. Each generation has a responsibility to invest in the next.

Jesus made this clear when He welcomed children and invited them to come to Him. In the same way, as we age, God can use us to lovingly warn younger generations about the dangers of a life lived without Christ at its center. Scripture gives sobering insight into what a Christless life can produce over time. Jeremiah describes the pain of a life marked by despair and hopelessness: *"He has made my skin and my flesh grow old and has broken my bones… He has made me dwell in darkness like those long dead"* (Lamentations 3:4–6, NIV). It's heartbreaking that many in the world grow old only to be consumed by bitterness and regret, when the answer to ageing with grace is found in Christ.

So what does a life with Christ at its center look like as we grow older? The apostle Paul gives us a beautiful picture. Writing to the Ephesians, he prayed that believers would *"know this love that surpasses knowledge—that you may be filled to the measure of all the fullness of God"* (Ephesians 3:19, NIV). A Christ-centered and Spirit-led life continues to grow fuller, not emptier, with time.

Paul also reminded the Galatians that a life rooted in Christ produces lasting fruit: *"The fruit of the Spirit is love, joy, peace, forbearance, kindness, goodness, faithfulness, gentleness and self-control"* (Galatians 5:22–23, NIV). These qualities do not diminish with age—they deepen. They reflect a life shaped by years of walking with God.

Peter adds yet another encouragement when he assures believers that perseverance in faith leads to a glorious conclusion: *"You will receive a rich welcome into the eternal kingdom of our Lord and Savior Jesus Christ"*

(2 Peter 1:11, NIV). Ageing with grace is not about clinging to youth; it's about growing in hope as eternity draws nearer.

As we grow older, we can know with confidence that we can age with grace and continue to bear fruit that pleases God. We can serve as examples of faithfulness, patience, and endurance. And we can play a vital role in training up the next generation *"in the way they should go" so that they will not depart from it* (Proverbs 22:6 NKJV).

Ageing with grace is not the end of usefulness. It can be a season where wisdom, faith, and legacy shine the brightest.

"Lord, as I grow older, help me to age with grace. Keep my heart tender toward You and my faith strong in every season of life. Show me how I can continue to bear fruit for Your glory and invest in the next generation. In Your name I pray, Amen."

THE IMPORTANCE OF HANDLING GOD'S WORD

The Word of God is one of the greatest gifts the Lord has entrusted to His people. It nourishes us, strengthens us, corrects us, and equips us to serve others faithfully. Yet Scripture also reminds us that how we handle God's Word matters deeply. When handled correctly, it brings life and growth; when handled carelessly, it can lead to confusion and spiritual harm.

The apostle Paul understood this well as he wrote to his young disciple Timothy. In a letter filled with pastoral concern and fatherly instruction, Paul emphasized the importance of properly handling the Word of God. At the heart of his instruction is this powerful exhortation: *"Be diligent to present yourself approved to God, a worker who does not need to be ashamed, rightly dividing the word of truth."* (2 Timothy 2:15, NKJV)

This verse has become a life verse for many believers, and for very good reason. It reminds us that God cares not only that we know His

Word, but that we handle it with care, integrity, and accuracy. This verse reference is engraved on the podium in the chapel at the New Brunswick Bible Institute, where I graduated from. I'm sure the staff wants to always remind their students and everyone who visits the campus just how important it is to handle the word of God correctly.

First, Paul tells us that we must be diligent with the Word of God. The word "*study*" in the older translations does not primarily refer to academic study, but to diligence and effort. The Greek word ***spoudazō*** carries the idea of being earnest, zealous, and persistent in accomplishing a task. Handling God's Word is not casual work—it requires focus, discipline, and reverence.

To be diligent means we approach Scripture thoughtfully, not carelessly. We need to read it prayerfully, allowing it to shape our thinking and correct our attitudes. We are not to be negligent with it, but cautious and attentive, knowing that this is God's revealed truth. Diligence with the Word should also spill into every area of our lives—our speech, our conduct, our relationships, our service, and our witness.

Paul also reminds us that diligence has a purpose: that we may be found "*approved to God.*" The word "*approved*" refers to something that has been tested and found acceptable. God sees all things and knows all things. Our goal is not to gain the approval of people, but to live in a way that pleases Him. As Paul asked the Galatians, "*Do I now persuade men, or God?*" (Galatians 1:10 NKJV) Our diligence should always be guided by a desire to honour the Lord.

Second, Paul teaches that we must be diligent workmen with the Word of God. The imagery here is of a labourer carefully completing a task. As believers, we are all workers in God's field. One day, we will stand before the Lord and give an account of our lives. On that day, we will either stand confident or ashamed.

John writes, "*And now, little children, abide in Him, that when He appears, we may have confidence and not be ashamed before Him at His coming*" (1 John 2:28, NKJV). Every day presents us with a choice—to live as faithful workers or careless ones. A diligent worker invests time in God's Word and seeks to apply it personally before sharing it with others. A careless worker may stay busy with religious activity but has little spiritual depth to offer.

Our desire should be to one day hear our Master say, "*Well done, good and faithful servant*" (Matthew 25:21, NKJV). That commendation comes from faithfulness, not perfection.

Finally, Paul reminds us that we must be diligent in our accuracy with the Word of God. He uses the phrase *"rightly dividing the word of truth,"* which means to handle Scripture accurately and responsibly. God's Word is not to be twisted to fit personal opinions or cultural trends.

Paul warns Timothy to avoid pointless arguments, godless chatter, and false teaching that only lead people away from the truth (2 Timothy 2:14, 16). False doctrine is dangerous because it undermines faith and confuses believers. That is why Paul was not hesitant to name false teachers and confront error. Truth matters because lives and eternity are at stake.

God's Word leads people to salvation. *"Faith comes by hearing, and hearing by the word of God"* (Romans 10:17, NKJV). If people are to come to a saving faith in Jesus Christ, then we must be diligent with the Word, faithful as workers, and accurate in how we teach and live it out.

> *"Lord, thank You for the precious gift of Your Word. Help me to handle it with diligence, humility, and accuracy. Guard my heart from carelessness or pride, and teach me to live what I learn. May I be a worker who is approved by You, not ashamed, and faithful until the day I stand before You, and may the Spirit guide me in using Your Word to point others to Christ, Amen".*

BECOMING BETTER NOT BITTER

Read: Acts 27

Most of us have experienced what sailors call a "sudden squall." The sky is calm, the waters seem manageable, and then, without warning, the wind shifts, the waves rise, visibility drops, and you lose control. In life, storms often arrive the same way. A phone call, a diagnosis, a conflict, a loss—suddenly what felt steady becomes uncertain. In those moments, we are forced to ask an important question: Will this storm make me bitter, or will it make me better?

Acts 27 records one of the most intense storms in Scripture. The apostle Paul, though innocent and obedient to God's call, finds himself caught in a violent Mediterranean storm while being transported to Rome as a prisoner. This was not a storm of his making. Yet, it became a defining moment of faith, leadership, and spiritual growth—not only for Paul, but for everyone aboard the ship. Today, we will look at some important takeaways from Acts 27 and this storm.

Courage in the Storm

Early in the voyage, Paul warned the crew that trouble lay ahead (Acts 27:10 NLT), but his counsel was ignored. When the storm struck, fear quickly took over. After days without sunlight or hope, Paul stood up and spoke words of courage: *"Take heart! For I believe God. It will be just as he said"* (Acts 27:25, NLT).

Courage does not mean the absence of fear; it means choosing to act in faith in the presence of fear. Scripture reminds us, *"For God has not given us a spirit of fear and timidity, but of power, love, and self-discipline"* (2 Timothy 1:7, NLT). In our storms, God calls us not to panic, but to trust His promises.

Protecting Character and Integrity

Storms have a way of revealing who we really are. Life's pressures expose our priorities, and fear will test our integrity. Paul's character remained steady even as the ship fell apart. He did not blame, manipulate, or despair. Instead, he served and encouraged others.

(Proverbs 11:3 NLT) says, *"Honesty guides good people; dishonesty destroys treacherous people"* NLT. Trials may strip away comfort and control, but we must never allow them to strip away our character. We must let our storms refine us, not ruin us.

Valuing Community in Crisis

Acts 27 makes it clear: Paul did not face the storm alone. Though a prisoner, he became a trusted voice. He urged the men to eat, to stay together, and not abandon the ship (Acts 27:31–36). Scripture tells us, *"Two people are better off than one, for they can help each other succeed"* (Ecclesiastes 4:9, NLT). God will often deliver strength, wisdom, and comfort through others, so do not withdraw—reach out.

Learning Through the Storm

Storms are not meaningless interruptions; they are often classrooms. Paul learned obedience, patience, and leadership in hardship. In the same way, God uses the trials in our lives to shape us. James writes, *"When troubles come your way, consider it an opportunity for great joy. For you know that when your faith is tested, your endurance has a chance to grow"* (James 1:2–3, NLT). We may not choose our storms, but we can choose how we grow through them.

Trusting God's Presence and Purpose

At the height of the storm, Paul received reassurance from God: *"Don't be afraid, Paul… God in his goodness has granted safety to everyone sailing with you"* (Acts 27:24, NLT).

God's presence did not prevent the storm, but it guaranteed Paul's purpose. Scripture consistently reminds us, *"The Lord himself goes before you and will be with you. He will never leave you nor forsake you"* (Deuteronomy 31:8, NLT). When we trust that truth, our expectations can shift from despair to hope.

From Misery to Mission

Remarkably, the storm positioned Paul for future ministry. His calm faith influenced soldiers, sailors, and prisoners alike. What began as misery became a mission. Romans 8:28 assures us, *"God causes everything to work together for the good of those who love God"* (NLT). This means that your storm may be the platform God uses to display His grace through you.

> *"Father God, thank You for being with me in every storm of life. When fear rises, and the winds are strong, help me to trust Your promises and rest in Your presence. Teach me what You want me to learn, and use my trials for Your glory. I will choose today not to become bitter, but better, by Your grace. In Jesus' Holy name I pray, Amen."*

THE POWER OF THE PROMISE

Waiting is rarely easy because most of us are often impatient. When we are asked to wait on God, questions often rise within our hearts. Will God really do what He said? Have I misunderstood His promise? Is it meant for me, or for someone else? Scripture repeatedly assures us that God is faithful, and when He makes a promise, it is always worth waiting for. God's promises are never empty words; they are certain, purposeful, and fulfilled in His perfect time.

After His resurrection, Jesus spent forty days speaking with His disciples about the kingdom of God. Before ascending into heaven, He gave them a clear instruction: "*I am going to send you what my Father has promised; but stay in the city until you have been clothed with power from on high*" (Luke 24:49, NIV).

The disciples were eager to move forward, yet Jesus called them to wait. Their waiting was not passive or pointless—it was preparation.

God was about to do something far greater than they could ever imagine.

In Acts 1:8, Jesus revealed the purpose of the promise: "*But you will receive power when the Holy Spirit comes on you; and you will be my witnesses in Jerusalem, and in all Judea and Samaria, and to the ends of the earth*" (NIV). The promise of the Holy Spirit was not merely for personal encouragement; it was for bold witness. God's power would enable ordinary men and women like you and me to proclaim an extraordinary message to the world.

This promise was something new. Centuries earlier, the prophet Joel spoke of a day when God would pour out His Spirit on all people (Joel 2:28–32). On the Day of Pentecost, Peter declared that what the crowd was witnessing was the fulfillment of that ancient promise. God's plan had been unfolding across generations, and now the moment had arrived. God always keeps His word, even when the fulfillment takes longer than we expect.

Jesus had prepared His disciples for this gift. In (John 14:26 NIV), He said, "*But the Advocate, the Holy Spirit, whom the Father will send in my name, will teach you all things and will remind you of everything I have said to you*". Later, He explained why His departure was necessary: "*Unless I go away, the Advocate will not come to you; but if I go, I will send him to you*" (John 16:7, NIV).

The Holy Spirit would continue the work Jesus began—guiding, teaching, convicting, and strengthening believers. Learning to listen to the Spirit requires spiritual attentiveness and a willing heart, but God is faithful to guide those who seek Him.

Acts 2:32–33 confirms that Jesus, now exalted to the right hand of God, received the promised Holy Spirit from the Father and poured Him out on the believers. The promise became visible and audible. What began in a small upper room spilled out into the streets of Jerusalem and around the world.

Peter's sermon that day cut straight to the heart. The people were deeply moved and asked, "*What shall we do?*" (Acts 2:37, NIV). This is the right response when God's truth confronts us. God's promises are not merely meant to inform us; they are meant to transform us. Peter's answer was direct and hope-filled: "*Repent and be baptized, every one of you, in the name of Jesus Christ for the forgiveness of your sins. And you will receive the gift of the Holy Spirit*" (Acts 2:38, NIV). Then comes one of the most reassuring statements in Scripture: "*The promise is for you and your children and for all who are far off—for all whom the Lord our God will call"* (Acts 2:39, NIV). What a wonderful promise for us today.

As we wait on God's promises, we can do so with confidence knowing that His timing is perfect, His purposes are good, and His power is still at work. The same Spirit who filled the early believers is available to us now. Let us wait with hope, and live as joyful witnesses to the faithfulness of our promise-keeping God.

"Lord, thank you for being a God who always keeps Your promises. When waiting feels difficult, help me to trust Your timing and rest in Your faithfulness. Fill me afresh with Your Holy Spirit, that I may be led by Him with boldness, obedience, and joy. As I wait, may I be faithful to share Your love and truth with those You place in my path. In Jesus' name I pray these things, Amen."

BENEATH THE SURFACE

Read: Jonah 1:1-12

Have you ever played hide-and-seek? My granddaughter Millie loves to play when she comes to visit. "Let's play hide and seek, Papa," she'll say, and how can I resist? She takes the game very seriously, carefully choosing a spot she thinks I'll never find. Sometimes she hides behind the curtains with her feet still showing, or behind the chair while quietly giggling. And yet, even when she's "hidden," she keeps peeking out, wanting to be found. It's innocent fun—but it reminds me that hiding often reveals more than we intend.

It's all fun and games until we realize that, in life, hiding can turn into something deeper—a way of avoiding responsibility, ignoring conviction, or running from what God is asking us to face.

Jonah was doing exactly that. God gave him a clear command: go to Nineveh and preach repentance. Instead, Jonah boarded a ship headed in the opposite direction, bound for Tarshish. Jonah wasn't just running from a task—he was running from God. His attempt to hide beneath the surface of obedience didn't just affect him; it put the lives of the sailors in serious danger (Jonah 1:4–5).

This instinct to hide is nothing new. When Adam and Eve sinned, their first response was to hide from the presence of the Lord (Genesis 3:8, NLT). Jonah followed the same pattern—partial obedience, selective listening, and his misplaced confidence that distance could dull God's call.

As we reflect on Jonah's story, it's worth asking: What are we hiding from? Is it a sin we've justified, a relationship we're avoiding, forgiveness we've withheld, or doubts we're afraid to admit? We often believe that if we bury these things deep enough, they'll disappear. But hiding doesn't heal—it isolates. What we keep beneath the surface will quietly grow heavier over time.

Yet here is the gracious truth: God was not finished with Jonah, and He's not finished with us. Even in Jonah's rebellion, God pursued him—not with destruction, but with discipline and mercy. There is deep freedom in knowing that no matter how far we run, God is near, inviting us back with grace rather than condemnation (Psalm 139:7–10, NLT).

Eventually, Jonah reached the end of himself. From the belly of the great fish, he prayed, *"I cried out to the Lord in my great trouble, and he answered me"* (Jonah 2:2, NLT). When Jonah stopped hiding, God responded. Even in the darkness, God's mercy reached him.

Perhaps today God is asking you to stop playing hide-and-seek. What lies beneath the surface of your heart? God already sees it—and He's not asking you to reveal it so He can shame you, but so He can heal you.

Paul reminds us that we are one body, and *"if one part suffers, all the parts suffer with it"* (1 Corinthians 12:26–27, NLT). Our hidden struggles often spill over into others' lives. Obedience, on the other hand, brings blessing not just to us, but to those around us.

Let us invite God to search our hearts and gently bring into the light whatever we've tried to keep hidden. Like Jonah, we'll discover that surrender is not the end—it's always the beginning of restoration.

"*Heavenly Father, there are moments when I choose to hide instead of trust and to run instead of obey. Thank You that I cannot outrun Your love or escape Your presence. Search my heart and reveal anything I've kept beneath the surface. Give me the courage to surrender fully to You, knowing Your grace is greater than all my fears or failures. In Jesus' name I pray, Amen.*"

DAY 47

A LESSON FROM A DONKEY

Read: Mark 11:1-11

The triumphant entry of Jesus into Jerusalem, just a week before His sacrificial journey to the cross, remains a powerful and symbolic moment in Christian history. As we reflect on this event, we cannot overlook the humble creature that played a crucial role in this divine procession—the donkey. This seemingly ordinary animal, chosen by the King of Kings for this momentous occasion, holds valuable lessons for us today.

Reflecting on today's passage, we witness Jesus instructing His disciples to fetch a young donkey for His entry into Jerusalem. This deliberate choice of transportation reveals a profound aspect of Christ's character—His purposeful plan. Jesus, being the sovereign Lord, could have chosen any mode of entry, yet He specifically selected a donkey. Similarly, our lives are not random or purposeless; God has a plan for each one of us.

Jeremiah 29:11 (NIV) assures us, "*For I know the plans I have for you*," *declares the Lord*, "*plans to prosper you and not to harm you, plans to give you hope and a future.*" Just as Jesus had a plan for the donkey, God has a unique plan for every individual. The first lesson from the donkey is to recognize and embrace God's purpose for our lives.

Now, this particular donkey wasn't randomly chosen by the disciples; it was chosen and appointed for a specific role in Christ's entry. In the same way, John 15:16 (NKJV) reminds us that we are chosen and appointed by God: "*You did not choose Me, but I chose you and appointed you that you should go and bear fruit, and that your fruit should remain, that whatever you ask the Father in My name He may give you.*"

Our lives, like the donkey, are appointed for a purpose—to bear lasting fruit for the glory of God. Embracing this truth requires a willingness to be used by God, just as the donkey willingly served the King. The lesson here is clear: our lives gain profound meaning when surrendered to God's purpose.

It's also important to take note that the donkey in this passage was found tied, meaning it could not serve until it was set free. In the same way, many individuals remain bound by worldly influences, hindering them from experiencing the freedom found in Christ. Galatians 5:1 encourages believers to stand firm in the freedom Christ provides and not be burdened again by a yoke of slavery.

To truly serve the King of Kings and Lord of Lords, we must break free from the ties that bind us—whether they be cultural, societal, or personal. Christ calls us to live in the freedom He offers, which will allow His Spirit to guide and lead us. The lesson from the donkey is a challenge to examine our lives and ensure that we are walking in the freedom that Christ has provided.

We should also be reminded that the disciples played a pivotal role in bringing the donkey to Jesus. Similarly, we are commissioned to bring others to Christ. The Great Commission in Matthew 28:19 (NKJV) urges believers to, "*Go therefore and make disciples of all the nations, baptizing them in the name of the Father and of the Son and of the Holy Spirit.*"

Our responsibility and calling is to introduce people to Jesus, creating opportunities for the Holy Spirit to convict and transform their lives. The donkey, in its simple obedience, teaches us the importance of being conduits through which others encounter Christ.

I'd like to mention one final point before I conclude. The donkey, though unbroken, did not resist when Jesus sat upon it. This remarkable obedience demonstrates the power of Christ to control and use even the most unyielding aspects of our lives. It serves as a reminder that no one is beyond God's transforming grace.

With privilege comes responsibility, and the privilege of being chosen and appointed by God requires a willing heart to be used for His glory. The donkey's humble submission to Jesus challenges us to yield our lives entirely to the Lord, trusting His sovereignty over every aspect.

In conclusion, the donkey's role in Christ's triumphant entry into Jerusalem offers profound lessons for our Christian journey. May this significant event cause us to reflect on the plan God has for our lives, acknowledging that we are chosen and appointed to bear lasting fruit. May we break free from any ties that hinder us, actively bring others to Jesus, and maintain a willing heart for God's transforming work.

Just as Jesus triumphantly entered Jerusalem, may He triumphantly enter our hearts, our homes, and every area of our lives. In surrendering to His plan and His purpose, we can discover true freedom and the joy of being vessels through which His glory shines.

"Heavenly Father, like the donkey in today's devotion, I know that you have a plan and a purpose for me. Today, I want You to triumphantly enter every area of my life so I can be used by You. I surrender to You, and I want to bear fruit so that You will be glorified. Amen"

The Holy Spirit's Leading

Read: John 16:6-15

On October 31, 1517, Martin Luther took a bold step that would change the course of history. He posted his 95 Theses on the door of the Castle Church in Wittenberg, Germany, sparking the Protestant Reformation. Luther's unwavering faith, fuelled by the Holy Spirit, led to a movement that resulted in the translation of the Bible into various languages and transformed the Church. On Reformation Day, we should remember the Person and Ministry of the Holy Spirit and how His guidance and enablement empower us to follow God, even when it means stepping out of our comfort zones.

Let's begin by reminding ourselves that the Holy Spirit is not some sort of cosmic force but a distinct Person of the Trinity. Scripture confirms His personhood, as evident in passages such as John 16:13-15. Jesus refers to the Holy Spirit using masculine pronouns in Greek, indicating His personhood. Moreover, the Holy Spirit guides, speaks, testifies, reproves, commands, helps, creates, inspires, loves, and teaches, demonstrating His characteristics as a Person.

Now, the Holy Spirit is not only a Person but also God Himself. Various passages identify the Holy Spirit as God. Deuteronomy 32:12 references the Holy Spirit's guidance as that of the LORD. In Isaiah 6:8-10 and Acts 28:25-27, the Holy Spirit is called Adonai, the Creator, Comforter, and *"The God of Israel."* The Holy Spirit is consistently equated with God throughout Scripture. He is coequal with the Father and the Son, as seen in Matthew 28:19.

The Holy Spirit is the primary Author of the Holy Scriptures. Acts 1:16 and other passages tell us that the Spirit spoke through prophets and authors of the Bible. Isaiah 6:9 and Acts 28:25 show the Spirit's inspiration of Isaiah's prophecies. Scripture claims to be inspired by the Holy Spirit, establishing Him as the Author of God's Word.

For believers, the Holy Spirit plays an active role in their lives. In the New Testament, the Holy Spirit permanently indwells believers, a truth affirmed in Romans 8:9. The Holy Spirit convicts the unsaved, drawing them to Christ, revealing their sin, and offering salvation. When a person believes, the Holy Spirit regenerates them, granting new life, fellowship with God, spiritual blessings, and eternal life.

For Christians, being filled with and led by the Holy Spirit is not about sensational experiences but practical empowerment. Ephesians 5:18 commands believers to be continually filled with the Spirit. This *"filling"* enables us to navigate life's circumstances in accordance with God's will.

The Holy Spirit's Person and Ministry are crucial to our understanding of the Christian faith. So, in the years ahead, let's not look negatively on the 31st of October. Let us reflect on the bold steps taken by reformers like Martin Luther, who, led by the Holy Spirit, transformed the Church and left a lasting legacy. We, too, can be guided, convicted, and empowered by the Holy Spirit to boldly live out our faith and make a difference in this world. Whether we need to surrender our lives to Christ or seek the continuous filling of the Holy Spirit, let us remember that His presence and influence are indispensable to our Christian journey.

> *"Father, I want to be filled by the Holy Spirit so that I can do your will and serve You with boldness. I thank You for sending the Holy Spirit into my life. I pray that the Holy Spirit will guide me and empower me to live out my faith today and in the days ahead, Amen."*

Seize the Moment and Live Life to the Fullest

Read: Philippians 3:7-16

In life, opportunities arise when we least expect them. One day, a young soldier and his commanding officer got on a train together. The only available seats were across from an attractive young woman who was travelling with her grandmother. As they engaged in pleasant conversation, the soldier and the young woman kept eyeing one another; the attraction was obviously mutual. Suddenly, the train entered a tunnel, and the car became pitch-black.

Immediately, two sounds were heard: the *"smack"* of a kiss, and the *"whack"* of a slap across the face. The grandmother thought, "*I can't believe he kissed my granddaughter, but I'm glad she gave him the slap he deserved."* The commanding officer thought, "*I don't blame the boy for kissing the girl, but it's a shame that she missed his face and hit me instead."* The young girl thought, "*I'm glad he kissed me, but I wish my grandmother hadn't slapped him for doing it."* And as the train broke into the sunlight, the soldier could not wipe the smile off his face. He had just seized the opportunity to kiss a pretty girl and slap his commanding officer, and he had gotten away with both!

This is a humorous tale, but it holds a valuable lesson: we must take advantage of every opportunity and seize the moment.

As we journey through life, it's easy to become preoccupied with daily routines, deadlines, commitments, problems, and priorities. The distractions and obstacles we face often make it challenging to fully embrace each day. However, deep within us, there is a desire for life to be more than just average – we long for a life that is full and prosperous.

The Apostle Paul, in Philippians 3, offers a philosophy of life that can help us live with purpose and seize every moment, even amid life's busyness and distractions.

To do this, we all need to find our purpose. Life becomes more meaningful when we discover our primary purpose. Just as an ink pen's purpose is to write, every individual has a reason for existing. Secondary purposes, like being a good spouse, parent, or professional, are important, but understanding your main purpose is essential. Paul's main priority was to be like Jesus. His life's reason was to know Christ and be conformed to His image.

The word Christian really means *"Christ-like-one"*. This means Christians are called to be like Jesus, to grow in our relationship with Him, and to reflect His character in our everyday lives. When we embrace this purpose, our lives take on a new meaning.

When Christians find their purpose, they can't dwell on their past. Dwelling on past mistakes or hurts can hinder your present and future. Just as a pen that is out of ink cannot fulfil its purpose, you cannot reach your full potential while dwelling on the past.

Don't let your past define you. God forgives our sins and gives us a fresh start. We must let go of the past, embrace forgiveness, and move forward. Paul knew this; he did not dwell on his past as a persecutor of Christians but pressed on toward the goal.

Leaving the past behind, we must face the present. In the story of Lazarus' resurrection, we find an essential lesson about living in the present. Martha, Lazarus's sister, expressed her faith in Jesus. She believed that He was the Christ, not just in the past or the future, but in that very moment. She said, *"Yes, Lord, I believe,"* acknowledging her faith in the present.

Living in the present means putting your trust in Jesus, allowing Him to be involved in every aspect of your life, and taking life one day at a time. It's about seizing each moment and living it with purpose.

Today, why not make the choice to seize the moment and live life to the fullest? Embrace your calling to be like Jesus, release the past, and have faith in Jesus in the present. Opportunities to experience a meaningful life are all around us. Don't let them slip away. Just as God worked in Paul's life, He is ready to work in yours. Say, *"Yes, Lord, I believe,"* and seize this moment in time all for the glory of God.

> *"Lord, I know I can't dwell on my past sins, hurts, and problems. If I still harbour any, I give them to you today. Dwelling on my past will prevent me from living in the present for You. I don't want opportunities to glorify You today to slip away. May Your Spirit empower me to seize this day for your glory and honour, Amen."*

DAY 50

THIRSTING FOR CHRIST

Read: John 19:16-30

Water is essential for life. Yet, even knowing its importance, sometimes we neglect to drink enough of it. For many years of my life, I never had a desire to drink water on a regular basis. I didn't find it had any flavour. For me, I failed to appreciate water until I found myself parched on a hot summer day or in a desert of my own making. Just as our physical bodies need water to survive, our spiritual souls need the living water that Christ offers. Let's examine the significance of our spiritual thirst and the fulfilment we can find in Christ.

In John 19:28, we witness an intimate moment during Christ's crucifixion. He cried out, *"I thirst."* This cry reflects His human nature, as He experiences suffering and pain. As He bore the weight of our sins, His body became weak and parched. Physical suffering is part of the human condition, but Christ's thirst demonstrates His willingness to identify with us in our moments of agony.

Likewise, in our lives, we may face physical suffering and hardships. Christ understands this aspect of our existence, and His thirst on the cross reminds us that He shares in our pain. When we are physically suffering, we can turn to Him, knowing that He empathizes with our struggles.

Christ's journey to Earth involved setting aside the glory He shared with the Father in heaven to accomplish His mission of salvation. His cry on the cross demonstrates His longing for full restoration with the Father. In John 17:4-5, He prayed for the glory He had before the world began to be restored. As we live our lives, let us consider seeking restoration with our heavenly Father. Instead of focusing on mere resolutions, we can strive for a deeper relationship with God. Our prayer could echo Christ's words, expressing our desire to bring glory to the Father as we walk with Christ.

Christ's intense thirst for the salvation of a lost world brought Him from the glory of Heaven to the humility of human form. His mission to seek and save the lost (Luke 19:10) demonstrates His unwavering commitment to offering salvation to wayward humanity. Let us never forget that it's our calling to share His thirst for the lost souls around us.

Just as Christ faced opposition and persecution, we may encounter challenges in our mission to share the gospel. Yet, His determination serves as our model. We should seek to see people come to Christ by sharing His message with those who are lost.

On the cross, Christ was forsaken by God and those closest to Him. This abandonment marked a moment of deep anguish. Now, there may be times when we feel isolated and abandoned. I'm sure we have all experienced times like this. However, Christ's *"Thirst"* for fellowship reminds us that He desires a close relationship with us.

In Matthew 18:20, Jesus promised His presence when two or more gather in His name. Let us remember this promise and seek sweet fellowship with Christ. He is near, eager for us to draw to Him. We can remain close to Him through our struggles and difficulties, or will we scatter in fear, like the disciples?

As we journey through life, let's find inspiration in Christ's *"Thirst"* on the cross. We need to know that He *"Thirsted"* physically and spiritually, for full restoration with the Father, for the salvation of the lost, and for fellowship with us. He desires to bring His blessings into our lives.

We often need a reminder that our *"Thirsty"* Saviour is knocking at the door of our hearts, waiting for us to invite Him in. The question is, how will we respond to Him every morning? I hope we will open the door and let Him in, so He can satisfy our spiritual thirst.

> *"Heavenly Father, I want to thirst as You did. May I thirst daily to be in a right relationship with You, and to fellowship with You. I also ask the Holy Spirit to plant within me a thirst for lost souls so that others who don't know You will not be spiritually parched, Amen."*

THE GREATEST OF THESE IS LOVE

Read: Galatians 5:16-23

Today, we will focus on the first fruit of the Spirit, which is 'love.' To set the stage, let me share with you a powerful love story that encapsulates the essence of sacrificial love. Have you heard of Maria Dyer?

Maria, born in 1837 on the mission field in China to missionary parents, faced adversity early on. After losing both of her parents at a very young age, she was sent back to England and was raised by her uncle. Orphaned at a young age, she defied the odds, returning to China as a missionary at 16 and working at a girls' school. At 21, she married Hudson Taylor, a renowned figure in Christian ministry, and together they faced criticism and hardship. Maria once wrote, "*As to the harsh judgings of the world, or the more painful misunderstandings of our Christian brethren, I generally feel that the best plan is to go on with our work and leave God to vindicate our cause.*" Hudson and Maria had a total of nine children; only four would survive to adulthood. And Maria herself died of cholera at the young age of forty-three.

Maria's life, marked by sacrifice, love, and loss, reflects the love we are called to emulate.

In our contemporary world, self-absorption often prevails. People prioritize personal gain over giving, making it a crucial time for a renewal of sacrificial love. Maria's life echoes the love described in the fruit of the Spirit in Galatians 5. As we delve into the concept of love, let us first acknowledge the various dimensions of love present in the English language.

Unlike English, the Greek language, prevalent in the New Testament, uses distinct words for different types of love. Understanding these nuances is vital in comprehending the depth of love we are called to express. The four Greek words for love are:

Eros - Erotic love
Storge - Empathetic love
Philia - Friendly or brotherly love
Agape - Unconditional, sacrificial love

The love instructed by the Holy Spirit to produce in us, as outlined in Galatians 5, is Agape love. It is an unconditional and sacrificial love that transcends conditions and expectations.

The Greek word «*Agape*» is defined as *"the highest form of love,"* representing charity, the love of God for man and of man for God. This love, characterized by its unconditional nature, is the foundational element in the fruit of the Spirit and is reiterated as the greatest in 1 Corinthians 13:13.

Agape love mirrors the love Christ demonstrated by laying down His life for us. As denoted in (John 15:13 NLT), *"There is no greater love than to lay down one's life for one's friends."* Maria Dyer's story and the biblical illustration of a mother sacrificing herself for her son vividly depict the sacrificial nature of Agape love.

The importance of producing fruit, particularly the fruit of love, is underscored in Matthew 7:16-21. True disciples are recognized by their actions and the fruit they bear. It emphasizes that true Christians are obedient, not merely professing Christians. Love, as the primary fruit, becomes a defining characteristic of genuine discipleship.

To manifest the love outlined in Galatians 5, we must heed Paul's advice in verses 24-25. Those who belong to Christ Jesus must crucify their sinful nature daily, allowing the Holy Spirit to lead every aspect of their lives. This continuous sacrifice aligns with the command to walk in the Spirit daily, producing the fruit of love consistently.

As we reflect on the significance of Agape love, we are prompted to examine our lives and identify the fruit we bear. Love, as the greatest commandment, is not a mere suggestion but an imperative for all believers. Embracing a sacrificial, unconditional love requires daily surrender and a commitment to follow the leading of the Holy Spirit. Just as Maria Dyer's life exemplified this love, may we too become vessels of Agape, radiating love in a self-absorbed world.

"Father, I take this moment to examine my actions and motives. Is everything I do and say driven by agape love? If not, Lord, I want it to be. Convict me in the areas I need to change so that I will express this love to You and others. I want to be a holy living sacrifice for You today. Amen"

DAY 52

BEING FULLY COMMITTED

Read: Acts 2:32-41

Today's scripture centres around a critical theme: commitment. In a world plagued by wavering loyalties, our commitment to various aspects of life, including marriage, family, friendships, work, and faith, often falters. This is evident even within the Christian faith, where believers sometimes struggle to uphold their commitments to Christ and the Great Commission.

Psalm 37:5 sets the tone, urging us to commit everything to the Lord. This isn't a selective commitment; it includes our cares, desires, needs, burdens, hopes, dreams, and plans. Our teaching today is about embracing this commitment wholeheartedly. In other words, being fully committed to the cause of Christ.

In today's passage, we see Peter passionately fulfilling his commitment to the Great Commission. His Spirit-filled message pierces hearts, leading people to ask the crucial question, *"What should we do?"*

Peter's response was not to simply say a prayer. He made a profound call for his listeners to make a true commitment to Christ, which involved genuine repentance, a turning away from sin, and publicly declaring allegiance through baptism.

A concerning trend in many churches today is a decline in commitment. Research indicates a substantial number of churches are facing stagnation or decline. As we explore our commitment to the Church, we find that membership involves more than attendance. God calls his children to give their time, gifts, and finances. The story of the poor widow's sacrificial giving in Mark 12 highlights the essence of generosity stemming from the heart. The challenge is clear: are we committed to supporting our church, understanding the significant impact it can have on ministry and outreach?

Jesus issues the Great Commission in Matthew 28, calling every Christian to make disciples. A simple equation illustrates the process: You + 1 (someone you lead to Christ) = 2, fostering church growth. However, a disturbing current trend is emerging: a lack of commitment to evangelism and discipleship. The equation now reflects a diminishing church—80 becoming 79, 79 becoming 74, and so on. Does this trend indicate a need for renewed commitment to the Great Commission?

Commitment to Christ, His Church, and the Great Commission is a collective effort. While some may excel in commitment, others may struggle. The key is acknowledging that true commitment is impossible in our own strength. The filling of the Holy Spirit and His leading is the answer. Ephesians 5:18 commands believers to *"Be filled with the Spirit."* This is not a suggestion, but rather a command. Oswald J. Smith emphasizes that being filled with the Spirit is the most important command when he said in his book *Enduement By Power*, *"This, you see, is a command — 'Be filled with the Spirit.' As a matter of fact, it is the most important commandment in the Bible. Because, you see, when you obey this commandment you automatically obey all the others. The fullness of the Spirit settles every problem in your life."*

Now, picture your life as a simple glass placed before the Lord. When it is empty, it represents a heart ruled by self—our own desires, plans, and distractions. As the glass is slowly filled with water, there is less room for anything else to remain. In the same way, when we yield ourselves to the Holy Spirit, His presence begins to fill every part of us, quietly displacing pride, selfish ambition, and our fleshly desires.

This reminds us that the Christian life is not merely about having the Spirit within us, but about allowing the Spirit to have full control over us. Every day we are invited to be filled again, so that how we walk, worship, serve, and give flows naturally from His indwelling presence. When the Holy Spirit fills our hearts, our commitment is no longer driven by duty, but becomes a joyful response of love and gratitude to the One who lives within us.

So, in conclusion, being fully committed requires more than our efforts; it demands the empowering and leading of the Holy Spirit. As we yield to His control, our commitment deepens, enabling us to fulfil our purpose in Christ. May we all seek to be filled with the Spirit, allowing Him to guide and empower our commitment to Christ today and for the rest of our days.

> *"Father, I want to be filled with the Holy Spirit so I can be fully committed to You and Your plan for my life. I surrender myself, and with Your help and in Your power, I want to help build Your kingdom and bring You glory. Amen"*

Ending Christian Intolerance

Read: Romans 14:1-13

In today's world, the buzzword is tolerance. We are surrounded by a culture obsessed with the concept of tolerance, yet, as Christians, we often find ourselves struggling to embody it within our own community. The Bible, however, offers us a guide to navigating the intricate landscape of tolerance within the Church. Today, we are exploring Romans 14:1-13, where Paul addresses tolerance among believers and how we can end Christian intolerance.

The first verse of our passage (Romans 14:1 NLT) sets the stage for understanding the principle of tolerance within the Christian community: "Accept other believers who are weak in faith, and don't argue with them about what they think is right or wrong." The term *"accept"* here implies more than mere tolerance; it encourages genuine, welcoming embrace without hidden agendas.

As followers of Jesus, God calls us to promote tolerance among

Christians on disputable matters. These *"disputable matters"* are honest differences of opinion among Bible-believing Christians about how best to apply biblical principles. It is crucial to note that Paul does not advocate tolerance in essential doctrines or clear moral absolutes; instead, he focuses on the non-essentials.

In verses 2 and 3, Paul provides an example to illustrate what qualifies for tolerance: the disagreement between those who eat anything and those who eat only vegetables. This example highlights that disputable matters arise from honest differences in applying biblical principles, not from compromising moral absolutes.

Paul offers several reasons for practising tolerance among believers:

1. Intolerance underestimates God's power. (14:4) Believers, both weak and strong, will stand with the Lord's help. Tolerance fosters perseverance and spiritual growth.

2. Intolerance undermines people's personal convictions. (14:5) Disputable matters often stem from personal convictions, and intolerance can lead to confusion and stumbling for others.

3. Intolerance questions people's motives. (14:6) Different practices, like worship styles or dietary choices, can all be done to honour the Lord. Intolerance hinders understanding and unity.

4. Intolerance minimizes Christ's Lordship.(14:8-9) All aspects of life, including disputable matters, fall under Christ's authority. Intolerance diminishes the comprehensive scope of Christ's lordship over believers' lives.

5. Intolerance usurps God's role in people's lives. (14:10-12) Every believer will one day stand before God's judgment seat individually. Intolerance disrupts unity and attempts to take on the role that belongs to God alone.

In conclusion, the biblical principle of tolerance applies to honest differences of opinion among Bible-believing Christians on non-essential matters. The focus is on disputable issues that arise from diverse convictions in applying biblical principles. However, the call goes beyond mere tolerance. Jesus challenges us to love one another sacrificially, to embrace and serve each other, and to extend love even to those with different convictions.

By practising Christian tolerance and, more importantly, embodying Christ-like love, we can end Christian intolerance. Let the world see our love for one another, a love that goes beyond mere tolerance, and declares the transformative power of Christ in our lives.

> *"Lord, I know that there is a vast array of differences and opinions within Your Church. By the power of Your Holy Spirit, I pray that I will embrace my brothers and sisters even though we may not agree on the non-essentials of the faith. Please allow me to do all I can to keep unity within the body of Christ so that You will be honoured and glorified. Amen"*

GOD'S PROMISE FOR PROTECTION

Read: Isaiah 41:1-20

In the midst of life's challenges and times of uncertainty, we often find ourselves wrestling with fear and doubt. The world bombards us with messages that can lead to what some call "stinkin thinkin" – negative thoughts that contradict what God says about us. In this devotion, we'll explore the contrast between our thoughts and God's promises, focusing on His assurance of protection found in Isaiah 41:10.

Let's start by acknowledging the stark contrast between our thoughts and God's promises, as illustrated below:

- We say: *"I can't do it."* God says: *"You can do all things through Christ." (Philippians 4:13)*

- We say: *"It's impossible."* God says: *"All things are possible." (Matthew 19:26)*

- We say: *"I'm too tired."* God says: *"Come to me, I will give you rest." (Matthew 11:28)*

- We say: *"I feel alone."* God says: *"I will never leave you or forsake you."* Hebrews 13:5)
- We say: *"I can't go on."* God says: *"My grace is sufficient for you."* (2 Corinthians 12:9)
- We say: *"I'm afraid."* God says: *"Fear not!"* (365 times in the Bible, depending on your version, or so I've heard.)

In 2 Timothy 1:7, Paul emphasizes that God has not given us a spirit of fear but of power, love, and self-discipline. Understanding this truth is vital as we reflect on God's promise of protection.

Now, before we proceed, I would like you to meditate on the following verse for just a few moments. Imagine God speaking this verse directly to you and over your life. *"Don't be afraid, for I am with you. Don't be discouraged, for I am your God. I will strengthen you and help you. I will hold you up with my victorious right hand."* (Isaiah 41:10 NLT)

With this verse fresh in your mind, let's explore God's Five Promises for Protection:

I Am With You:

It is comforting to know that God is constantly with His children. In John 14:16, Jesus assures us that the Holy Spirit, our Advocate, will never leave us. Whether in good times or bad, God's presence remains a source of peace beyond understanding.

I Am Your God:

God encourages us not to be discouraged or dismayed. The Hebrew translation reveals that discouragement often arises when we look around rather than keeping our gaze upward. Confidently affirming that *"He is our God, and we will not be shaken"* (Unknown) helps us maintain focus and avoid discouragement.

I Will Strengthen You:

God's promise to strengthen His people is crucial, especially in times of weakness. Acknowledging our weaknesses, as Paul did in 2 Corinthians 12:10, allows God's strength to manifest. When we are strengthened by God, *"All things are possible,"* and no task is too difficult.

I Will Help You:

The Hebrew word for help, ***"aw-zar,"*** implies God's active involvement in aiding, surrounding, and protecting us. As we work in cooperation with God, He assists, guides, and protects us in our endeavours. His help comes precisely when needed, aligning with His perfect timing.

I Will Hold You:

God promises not only to hold us but to hold us up with His victorious right hand, symbolizing His power and strength. Isaiah 48:13 highlights the magnitude of God's power, emphasizing that once securely in His hand, no one can snatch us away. In times of uncertainty and difficulty, we will find security in His firm grasp.

In a generation marked by fear and uncertainty, God's promises stand as beacons of hope and assurance. As Christians, we can take comfort in God's repeated command: *"Fear not, for I am with you."* His promise for protection encompasses the assurance that He is our God, able to strengthen, help, and hold us securely in His victorious right hand.

Understanding and applying these promises to our lives will shelter us beneath God's wings, protect us through His power, and provide for us through His unfailing love. Let us stand firm on this promise, recognizing that our God is faithful and His protection is our refuge.

> *"Father, I don't want to live in fear knowing that You are always with me. In times of uncertainty, I want to stand on the promises of God my Saviour. And, I want to take comfort knowing that You hold me in Your hand and will never let me go. Amen"*

GOD'S PROMISE FOR PEACE

Read: John 14:15-27

Today, our scripture passage addresses a theme that resonates deeply within the human heart—peace. As we navigate the challenges of life, the pursuit of peace often feels elusive, both on a personal and global scale. We see the struggles for peace in statistics, such as the alarming number of wars and lives lost throughout recorded history. In a world desperate for peace, we find solace in God's promise. As we study our passage today, we will uncover the timeless truths about God's provision of peace.

It is no secret that we live in a world marred by conflict and discord; the pursuit of peace is a universal desire. However, many search for peace in people, places, and possessions, only to find it fades. The pursuit of worldly solutions often leads to disappointment, as Ecclesiastes 2:10-11 highlights, where even the wise King Solomon found his longing for peace through knowledge and wisdom to be meaningless.

The primary reason for the world's lack of peace is sin, which separates and alienates people from God. As Isaiah (48:22, NKJV) asserts, *"There is no peace, says the Lord, for the wicked."* Peace and rebellion against God cannot coexist. It's crucial to understand that true peace can only be found by aligning our lives with God's will.

Amid the chaos, God provides a solution to achieving peace through the sacrifice of His Son, Jesus Christ. Colossians 1:20 declares that through Christ's blood on the cross, God reconciled everything to Himself, bringing peace to both heaven and earth. Jesus' promise of peace in John 14:27 comes during a critical moment in His earthly ministry, emphasizing its significance.

Theologian Joseph Henry Thayer provides a poignant definition of peace, describing it as *"the tranquil state of a soul assured of its salvation through Christ and so fearing nothing from God, and content with its earthly lot whatever sort it be."* Jesus exemplifies this peace, facing His impending betrayal and the cross with a serene confidence rooted in harmony with God's will.

Let's look at three Factors of God's Promise for Peace:

The pursuit of God's peace (John 14:15-27) begins with recognizing the spiritual separation caused by sin. Pursuing worldly solutions or pleasure, as Solomon discovered, cannot bring lasting peace. Isaiah 53:5 and Ephesians 2:14 emphasize the need for reconciliation with God through Jesus Christ.

God's provision of peace (Colossians 1:20) is an outpouring of His grace, accomplished through Christ's sacrifice on the cross. Through faith in Jesus, we gain reconciliation with God and access to the peace that surpasses worldly understanding. This peace, unlike any other, is a gift that the world cannot replicate.

Possessing God's peace (Romans 5:1) is conditional on repentance and faith in Jesus Christ. Romans 5:1 reminds us that through faith, we gain peace with God. True and lasting peace is a possession of the believer, born out of a personal relationship with Christ.

In summary, the pursuit, provision, and possession of God's peace are intertwined with our relationship with Him. As we strive for peace in our lives, families, churches, and beyond, let's remember that true peace comes from God alone. The pursuit of peace necessitates a turning away from sin and acknowledging our need for reconciliation with God.

God's provision of peace, made possible through the sacrificial love of Jesus, transcends the temporal and reaches into the eternal. It's a gift that surpasses anything the world can offer. Possessing this peace requires faith and trust in Jesus Christ, recognizing Him as the source of true and lasting peace.

So, let us be challenged to stay close to God, seeking unity with one another, and allowing the peace of Christ to rule in our hearts. As (Colossians 3:15, NLT) encourages us, *"Let the peace that comes from Christ rule in your hearts. For as members of one body, you are called to live in peace. And always be thankful."* May God's promise for peace be a guiding light in our lives and a testimony to the world.

"Heavenly Father, I want to live in peace and share Your everlasting peace with others. My desire is to pursue and possess Your peace that surpasses all of my understanding. So today, I seek Your forgiveness for anything that will hinder my peace with You. Amen"

DAY 56

GOD'S PROMISE OF HIS PRESENCE

Read: Exodus 33:12-23

As we live out our faith, there is a truth that echoes through the corridors of time—the promise of God's presence. Long before us, believers have testified to the nearness of God in moments of weakness and sorrow. A. H. Ackley captured this beautifully when he wrote, "In my failure, sin, and sorrow, brokenhearted, crushed and torn, I have felt His presence near me." That promise is not mere poetic sentiment; it's deeply rooted in Scripture. Today, we will pause to reflect on the reality of God's Promise of His Presence.

Our guide in this passage is Moses, the faithful servant of God, standing at a pivotal moment in Israel's history. In Exodus 33:12–23, Moses finds himself at a crossroads. The people have sinned grievously with the golden calf, and though God has forgiven them, He declares that He will send an angel ahead—but not go with them Himself. For Moses, that was unthinkable. With holy boldness, he pleads to God, "*If*

Your Presence does not go with us, do not bring us up from here" (Exodus 33:15, NKJV). God responds with a gracious assurance: "*My Presence will go with you, and I will give you rest*" (v.14).

Can you imagine the weight of that moment? Moses, hidden in the cleft of the rock, heard the Lord pass by and proclaim His name. Though Moses could not see God's face and live, he was granted a glimpse of God's glory. This encounter reminds us that God's presence is not abstract—it's personal, it's powerful, and it's transforming.

The promise of God's presence was given against the backdrop of failure and intercession. Israel had broken covenant, yet Moses stood in the gap. Scripture tells us that Moses spoke with God "*face to face, as a man speaks to his friend*" (Exodus 33:11 NKJV). His humility, obedience, and willingness to intercede made room for God's mercy to be displayed.

In our own lives, the background of God's promise is often similar. It's birthed not in perfection, but in repentance. When we turn from our sin, surrender our will, and seek the Lord with a sincere heart, we position ourselves to experience His nearness. God is not distant from the brokenhearted; He draws near to those who call upon Him in truth.

Today, we enjoy access to God's presence because of Christ. Hebrews reminds us that we have "*boldness to enter the Holiest by the blood of Jesus, by a new and living way… through the veil, that is, His flesh*" (Hebrews 10:19–20, NKJV). The torn veil stands as a permanent testimony to God's desire for fellowship with His people.

While church attendance, prayer, and spiritual disciplines are vital, they are not substitutes for a humble and repentant heart. Moses did not demand God's presence—he depended upon it. James echoes this truth when he writes, "*Draw near to God and He will draw near to you*" (James 4:8, NKJV). God's presence is promised, but it is fully experienced by those who walk in humility and obedience.

The presence of God also brings assurance, strength, and peace. It does not remove every trial, but it reminds us that we are never alone. Jesus said, "*No one shall snatch them out of My hand*" (John 10:28, NKJV). In His presence, we find rest for our souls and strength for the journey. Paul declared, "*I can do all things through Christ who strengthens me*" (Philippians 4:13, NKJV).

God's presence sustains us in uncertainty, steadies us in sorrow, and will strengthen us in our service. This is the difference between wandering aimlessly and walking confidently in the Spirit by faith.

Finally, the promise of God's presence remains a beacon of hope for every believer. The same God who walked with Moses, strengthened Joshua, encouraged Jeremiah, and stood by Paul now walks with you and me because of His promise to,…"*never leave you nor forsake you*" (Hebrews 13:5, NKJV).

May we, like Moses, refuse to move forward without Him. May we learn to value His presence above success, comfort, or security, and may our lives reflect hearts that are surrendered and eager to dwell in the nearness of our faithful God.

> *"Father in heaven, I thank You for the promise of Your presence. I confess my need for You in every season of life, especially in moments of weakness and uncertainty. Help me to repent where my heart has grown distant. Teach me to rest in the assurance that You will never leave me nor forsake me. In Jesus' name I pray, Amen."*

God Keep Our Land

Read: Revelation 4:1-11

The book of Revelation paints a vivid picture of the majestic throne of God, surpassing any earthly authority or power. In our passage today, we are exploring the profound implications of God's throne and considering what it means for our beloved land.

In Revelation 4:1-11, the Apostle John gives us a glimpse into the heavenly realm, where a door stands open, revealing the throne of God. The scene unfolds with heavenly creatures declaring, *"Holy, holy, holy is the Lord God Almighty."* The image of God's throne is one of majesty, power, and authority. It far surpasses any earthly throne, even the ceremonial Throne of Parliament in Canada or any other Government authority.

In the country where I was born, at the commencement of each parliamentary session, the Governor General delivers the Speech from the Throne. Yet, the power and authority expressed in this speech pales in comparison to the sovereignty emanating from God's heavenly throne.

Our world's mightiest military forces are nothing compared to the divine power of the Creator of the heavens and the earth.

Acknowledging the omnipotence of God, we recognize Him as the greatest Supreme Commander of all time. It is on His throne in Heaven that God, together with His Son Jesus, holds authority over all creation. By their power, the cosmos was formed, and all things find coherence. Redemption flows from God's power and authority, underscoring His supremacy in the grand tapestry of existence.

Every year on July 1st, we celebrate Canada Day in Canada. For the church, it's a day that should bring us an awareness that the blessings and freedoms we enjoy find their source in the benevolent rule of our heavenly King. For our neighbours to the South, an equivalent day would be the 4th of July or Independence Day. For Christians, these celebrations should be a reminder that our land is not governed merely by human institutions but is under the divine oversight of the Lord God Almighty.

If God were to deliver a *"Throne Speech"* or address the nation, what would be His agenda? In contemplating this question, we turn to His Word for guidance. One clear message emerges:

Much Given, Much Required

Reflecting on Luke 12:48, we are reminded that for everyone who is given much, much is required. My country, Canada, is a nation abundantly blessed. We enjoy freedom, prosperity, and a rich heritage. However, as stewards of God's blessings, we must respond with generosity and gratitude. God, who reigns on His heavenly throne, calls us to be faithful stewards of the abundant resources and freedoms bestowed upon us.

Repent and Return

Drawing from the lessons of Jeremiah and Isaiah, we hear the echoes of God's call to repentance. A nation that may outwardly profess faith can still be plagued by inner rebellion. Our collective hearts must be turned toward God, forsaking idols and selfish pursuits. The call to repent and return echoes through the corridors of time, urging us to align our national identity with the principles that recognize the supremacy of God.

God Can Heal Our Land

Amidst the challenges and struggles faced by our nation, a beacon of hope emerges from 2 Chronicles 7:14 (NKJV) where God says: *"If my people... will humble themselves and pray and seek my face and turn from their wicked ways, then I will hear from heaven, and I will forgive their sin and will heal their land."* The formula for healing begins with humility, prayer, repentance, and seeking God's face.

In my debut fiction novel, *Up From the Ashes, A Story of Healing, Hope and Second Chances*, one of the main characters, Clara, struggles with the challenges her country, the United States, faces amid the divisiveness. When her husband asks her if she has any solutions to their country's problems, she directs him to the verse above.

As we reflect on God's sovereign throne and His divine agenda for our country, let us respond with humility, gratitude, and a sincere commitment to live out our faith. Canada, along with many other nations, has a diverse tapestry of cultures and beliefs, and stands as a testament to God's creativity. Whatever country you live in, I would encourage you to pray for your leaders as you heed the call to repentance, embrace humility, and fervently seek the face of our Creator.

For all my fellow Canadians, when the next Canada Day rolls around, let our hearts echo the plea, *"God Keep Our Land, Glorious and Free,"* not merely as a patriotic anthem but as a genuine prayer for divine guidance, healing, and restoration.

> *"Father, I lift up my nation and its leaders to you today. May we be a nation that seeks your face and calls upon your name for healing and restoration, Amen."*

DAY 58

FINISHING THE RACE WITH THE FLAME STILL BURNING

Read: Philippians 3:12-16

Most races are measured by speed. The winner is the one who crosses the finish line first. But the Christian life is not a sprint, and it's not a competition against each other. It's a long-distance race of faith, endurance, and obedience. The question Scripture presses upon us is not simply, "Will you finish?" but more importantly, "How will you finish?"

The apostle Paul often described the Christian life as a race. Near the end of his life, he wrote, "*I have fought the good fight, I have finished the race, I have kept the faith*" (2 Timothy 4:7, NKJV). Paul's goal was not merely to survive spiritually, but to finish faithfully. He wanted to run in a way that honoured Christ from start to finish.

There is an ancient story from the early Olympic Games that helps frame this truth. In one particular race, the winner was not determined by who crossed the line first, but by who finished with their torch still lit. Speed mattered, but endurance mattered more. Guarding the flame was essential. That image speaks powerfully to the Christian life. Many believers begin their race with passion and clarity, but somewhere along the way, the flame begins to flicker. Paul challenges us to finish with our light still burning brightly.

In Philippians 3, Paul shares several essentials for running—and winning—this spiritual race. The first may surprise us: holy dissatisfaction. Paul writes, *"Not that I have already attained, or am already perfected; but I press on"* (Philippians 3:12, NKJV). Though mature in faith, Paul refused to settle into spiritual complacency. He was not discouraged, but he was honest. He knew there was more growth ahead. True maturity recognizes progress without pretending perfection.

From that dissatisfaction flows devotion. Paul continues, *"But one thing I do… I press toward the goal"* (Philippians 3:13–14, NKJV). The Christian life is often cluttered by distractions. We try to juggle too many priorities and wonder why progress feels slow. Paul's focus was singular. His devotion was centered on knowing Christ and becoming more like Him. The truth is that growth happens when faith is not divided.

Our devotion also gives direction. Paul says he was *"forgetting those things which are behind and reaching forward to those things which are ahead"* (Philippians 3:13, NKJV). Forgetting does not mean erasing the past, but refusing to let it control the present. Regrets, failures, and even past successes can hinder forward movement if we dwell on them. God promises, *"Their sins and their lawless deeds I will remember no more"* (Hebrews 10:17, NKJV). If God does not hold our past against us, neither should we.

Yet direction alone is not enough. Paul emphasizes determination. *"I press toward the goal for the prize of the upward call of God in Christ Jesus"* (Philippians 3:14, NKJV). The word press carries the idea of strain and effort. Paul knew the Christian life would involve resistance, sacrifice, and perseverance. Faith is not passive. Like an athlete in training, believers must stay engaged, committed, and disciplined.

That leads to the final essential: obedience through discipline. Paul urges believers to *"walk by the same rule, let us be of the same mind"* (Philippians 3:16, NKJV). Spiritual knowledge without obedience does not strengthen faith—it will weaken it. Discipline is simply choosing to live out what God has already shown us. One day, Scripture tells us, every believer will stand before the judgment seat of Christ (Romans

14:10–12). This is not a judgment of condemnation, but of reward. Like the ancient athletic games, faithfulness will be honoured.

Many in Scripture started strong but failed to finish well. Others ran steadily and finished with joy. The difference was not talent or opportunity; it was their faithfulness. Every day we are called to run our race with endurance, "*Looking unto Jesus, the author and finisher of our faith*" (Hebrews 12:2, NKJV). May we be found faithful—not just crossing the finish line, but doing so with our flame still burning.

> *"Heavenly Father, I thank You for calling me into this race of faith. Forgive me for the times I have grown complacent, distracted, or discouraged. Help me to press on with devotion and determination. I must leave the past behind and keep my eyes fixed on Christ because I want to finish well, with my faith burning bright for Your glory. In the name of Jesus, I pray, Amen."*

MAKING A DIFFERENCE

Read: Ecclesiastes 9:1-10

Today, we will be looking at how we can make a difference in this world. In our passage, Solomon warns and instructs us simultaneously, urging us to live purposefully and to make the most of the time we have.

Solomon begins by acknowledging the universal fate that awaits everyone—death. This reality, he suggests, should prompt people to be more careful to live good lives. However, many choose their own course, driven by a lack of hope. Solomon implies that when people put their hope in themselves, they tend to pursue self-centred and often futile paths.

Solomon contrasts the living and the dead, emphasizing that there is hope only for the living. The resurrection of the dead was not a common concept in the Old Testament. While the dead are forgotten and have no further reward, the living have the opportunity to make a lasting impact on earth. The teaching here is clear: our hope should come from the Lord.

So, if the teaching is that there is only hope for the living, let me ask, who are you putting your hope in? Continuing on in our passage, Solomon challenges us to reflect on where we place our hope. Our hope should not be in ourselves, our leaders, our countries, our government leaders, or worldly things, but in the Lord. Human sources of hope are fallible, but the Lord is steadfast. The role of leaders, like pastors, is not to be the source of hope but to direct people to place their hope in God.

I'd like to remind all of us that Solomon's message goes beyond a mere warning; it's a call to action. Despite the brevity of life, as discussed in another devotion, God has a significant plan for each one of us. The dead have no further reward, but the living have the opportunity to participate in God's work here on earth. Our mission is to make disciples, and we should embrace the possibilities and opportunities God presents.

Mission trips are among the many practical ways to make a difference. The desire is for individuals to return with a greater hope in the Lord and a deeper commitment to love and serve Him. Whether in Haiti or Costa Rica, both places I've served or led short-term mission teams, or our local community, allows us the opportunity to make a significant impact for His Kingdom.

The wisdom of Solomon encourages us to embrace the possibilities that God sets before us. Instead of being pessimistic or cynical, Christians should focus on the potential for positive change. God's grace abounds where sin increases, and we should be a people full of hope, fully trusting in God's plans.

Solomon's final instruction is to go and do well. It's a call to action, to walk, move forward, and live life to the fullest. We are reminded that whatever we do, we should do it well and for the glory of God. Philippians 2:13 emphasizes that God works in us, providing both the desire and the power to please Him.

Moving forward in faith with a desire to make a difference in this world begins with an awareness of life's brevity. From that perspective, we are called to place our hope and trust in God, to live every day fully, and to carry out our tasks with excellence for the glory of God.

In the days ahead, I challenge you to prayerfully commit the limited time we have into the Lord's hands. Even the smallest acts of service, when offered to Him, can carry eternal significance. As we walk in the

Spirit, let us place our trust in the Lord and seek to honour Him in all we do. And when our journey is complete, my hope and prayer is that we will hear His gracious words, *"Well done, my good and faithful servant."*

> *"Father, Solomon teaches us that life is short compared to eternity, and with the limited time I have left on this earth, I want to use it wisely. I want to love You and serve You with all my heart, and I want the rest of my life to be filled with purpose so that You will be glorified, Amen."*

DAY 60

PRESSING ON
(A TRIBUTE TO PASTOR JOHN MCLEAN)

Read: Hebrews 12:1-4

While serving as a Pastor for just under a decade, I had the great privilege to serve alongside my Assistant Pastor, John McLean, who has now gone home to be with the Lord. In his younger years, he was an avid runner, and when life and ministry were difficult, he would often encourage me and others to "Press On." So, I wanted to dedicate this devotion in his honour.

Our passage today tells us that the Christian life is like a marathon, not a sprint. As believers, we run with endurance, aiming to reach our highest potential, set a positive example for others, and ultimately bring glory to God. The race is not to attain salvation but to live a life of thankfulness and gratitude for the free gift of eternal life. However, our race will have challenges and difficulties. We know this because the Greek word for '*race*' in Hebrews 12:1 is '*agon*' and carries the idea of '*strife*', '*peril*', or '*toil*.' It's from this Greek word that we get the English word '*agony*.'

In this race, we strive to become the best version of ourselves, living for Jesus and reaching our highest personal potential. The focus is on personal growth and fulfilment, not competition with others.

We also run the race to set a positive example for others. Our lives should reflect Christ's love and inspire those around us to seek Him. As Christians, we carry the responsibility of being positive influences in the lives of those whom God places on our path.

Our ultimate goal is to glorify God in everything we do. 1 Corinthians 10:31 reminds us to do all things for the glory of God, including running the race with endurance.

The first-century Christians addressed in Hebrews faced challenges, including persecution and societal rejection. Today, believers still encounter difficulties, both in day-to-day life and through the opposition of Satan. Despite these challenges, the race is one worth running.

Life brings its share of struggles to us all, and as Christians, we are not exempt from facing difficulties. However, with the Lord's strength, we can overcome all our obstacles.

Satan, though defeated, seeks to make believers miserable and hinder their spiritual growth. Christians are encouraged to resist him steadfastly in faith, relying on the Lord's power to overcome.

Reflecting on today's scripture reading, we see that the writer of Hebrews provides a strategic plan for running and winning the race that God has set before all His children.

Firstly, let's **reflect** on the faith and endurance of those who came before us. I don't believe I will ever forget the deep, rich faith of Pastor John McLean and the legacy he has left behind. When the Lord brings him to mind, my faith is encouraged. Now, the great cloud of witnesses mentioned in Hebrews 12:1 refers to the heroes of faith listed in chapter 11. Their examples inspire and encourage us to press on despite difficulties. When you are facing difficult times, returning to Hebrews 11 or remembering the faith of those who have touched your life in the past may help remind you that even the greatest heroes in history struggled as we do.

Secondly, to run this race successfully, believers are instructed to lay aside every weight and sin. Weights could be anything hindering our walk with Christ, and sin, no matter how easily entangling, must be cast aside. Vigilance, prayer, and staying in God's Word help us resist sin.

Finally, the ultimate strategy for victory is to fix our eyes on Jesus, the author and finisher of our faith. Jesus endured the cross, despising the shame, and now sits at the right hand of God. He is our supreme example and source of strength.

So, as we navigate the challenges of life, let's remember the strategy outlined in Hebrews 12:1-4. By considering those who came before us, laying aside weights and sin, and staying focused on Christ, we can press on in hard times. In John 16:33, Jesus assures us that in this world, we will face tribulation, but in Him, we find peace and victory.

> *"Lord, may today's devotion remind me that I will face trials and tribulations. My prayer is that when trouble comes, I will look to those who have finished their race well, such as the heroes of the faith described in Hebrews 11. And then may I lay aside every weight and sin, and fix my eyes upon You, Amen."*

Fighting the Good Fight

Read: Ephesians 6:11-18

Today's devotion is written from notes I took during a message my son Ryan Ranni preached at his church on December 31st, 2023. As one of the pastors on staff, Ryan wanted to remind the congregation that, as they entered a new year, they would need to stand firm against the schemes of the enemy. The truth he preached that day is a helpful reminder to all believers.

Looking at our text, the first thing Ryan shared was that, as followers of Christ, we must recognize our adversary (Ephesians 6:11-13). The Scriptures teach us that our battle is not against flesh and blood, but against spiritual forces of evil. The devil's schemes include chaos, confusion (Jonah 4:1), and compromise (Genesis 3:1). R. Kent Hughes said, "*he (the devil) knits just enough good with evil to achieve his purposes.*" With this in mind, we are called to be discerning, not ignorant of his designs, understanding that he seeks to distract us from God's purpose.

By knowing our enemy and staying rooted in God's Word, we can withstand his attacks and stand firm in the faith.

Secondly, to fight the good fight, we must be equipped with the whole armour of God (Ephesians 6:14-18a). This includes the belt of truth, breastplate of righteousness, shoes of the gospel of peace, shield of faith, helmet of salvation, and the sword of the Spirit, which is the Word of God. Our personal devotion to Jesus through His word is the key to being equipped daily. A.J. Higgins put it this way, "*The secret of the Christian life is the secret Christian life.*" We all need to be equipped with the word of God so we can fight with a sharp blade. Jesus is our example here. In Matthew 4:3-11, Jesus is tempted three times by Satan, and with every temptation, Jesus fought back using the word of God by saying, "*It is written.*"

Thirdly, the call to fight for the Lord is a call to fight faithfully. Our passage reminds us to always be vigilant and alert, standing up for Christ and fighting for Him in every area of our lives (Ephesians 6:18b). During my son's message, he used an illustration. He looks to the soldier who goes through their training and is given a post or position and uniform, but it is only then that the duty begins. I've experienced this firsthand during my nineteen years in the military. In the same way, followers of Jesus are trained, equipped, and posted, and their duty is to be faithful in the fight.

It's the local church that serves as the barracks where we are trained, encouraged, and equipped, with the world as our battlefield where we fight for the kingdom of light. Our churches are filled with husbands, wives, parents, children, grandparents, aunts, uncles, leaders, influencers, doctors, lawyers, teachers, mechanics, etc. We have been given our postings, and we are called to remain faithful to fight the good fight where we have been placed. We can so easily take our position for granted or lose sight of our calling. Still, God's word reminds us that we are in a war that is raging, and we are called to stand firm and fight for the kingdom because the reward is worth it! (James 1:12)

As I close this devotion, let us remember that fighting for the kingdom is a call to fight for the King; we are to remain faithful at our posts. The enemy seeks to lull us into sleep and cause us to forget our responsibilities, but we must stay vigilant and pray for one another. Our Master will return, and we must be found ready, dressed for action, and serving faithfully. (Luke 12:35-40) May we be holy, blameless, and faithful, all for the glory of our King Jesus.

> *"Lord Jesus, you have called me to be a soldier in your army. Each and every day, I must be equipped with the armour of God and be prepared to fight the good fight. I ask you today to strengthen me and prepare me for the battles in which I must fight so that I will be faithful and you will be glorified, Amen."*

TRUSTING THE WORD OF GOD

Read: 2 Timothy 4:1-14

In the previous devotion, there was a strong emphasis on the Word of God. So, I thought it fitting that in this devotion we focus on God's Word and learn why and how we can have complete trust in it.

In a world swayed by diverse opinions and ever-changing ideologies, the Word of God stands as an unshakeable foundation. It's not merely a collection of stories and verses but a revelation of divine truths that pierce through the fog of confusion and lead us into the radiant light of God's wisdom. Within this sacred text, we find guidance, conviction, and a transforming power that can shape our lives.

The apostle Paul, in his letter to Timothy, urges believers to *"Preach the word of God"* (2 Timothy 4:2 NLT). I remember the first time I preached from the pulpit in the church I pastored. I noticed something etched into the pulpit on my side that the people didn't see. Only the one preaching saw the phrase, *'Preach the Word and love the people'*. This charge to preach the word is not confined to a specific time or situation; rather, it's a timeless universal command. The urgency of preaching the Word is emphasized as Paul foresees a time when people will turn away from sound teaching and follow their own desires, seeking messages that align with their own preferences (2 Timothy 4:3-4). In the face of this challenge, Paul encourages the unwavering proclamation of God's truth.

To be confident in the Word of God, every believer needs to know that the Bible is more than a compilation of ancient writings. It's the living Word of God, a powerful force that cuts through the depths of our being. Hebrews 4:12 vividly describes the potency of the Word: *"It is sharper than the sharpest two-edged sword, cutting between soul and spirit, between joint and marrow. It exposes our innermost thoughts and desires."* The Word is not just a record of revelation but the revelation itself, preserved for eternity.

To build our trust in the Word of God, today we will look at the revelation of the Word, the inspiration of the Word, and the illumination of His Word, so let's begin.

Revelation is the unveiling of divine truth. It brings to light truths that were previously hidden or obscure. God, in His wisdom, communicated with humanity through various means, including visions, dreams, and direct encounters. The written Word is a tangible form of this revelation, allowing us to accurately receive and preserve God's truth. The scriptures are God's revealed truth in written form, a divine gift that unveils the mysteries of His nature and His purpose.

While revelation is a supernatural act, inspiration involves the recording of God's truth by human hands. The apostle Peter affirms that the prophets who recorded God's Word were moved by the Holy Spirit (2 Peter 1:20-21). The Bible declares that all scripture is inspired by God (2 Timothy 3:16). The very word *"inspired"* denotes being *"God-breathed."* This divine influence ensured the flawless transmission of God's message from the hearts of individuals to the pages of scripture.

Consider the profound truth captured in (Psalm 33:6, NLT): *"The LORD merely spoke, and the heavens were created. He breathed the word, and all the stars were born."* If God, with a mere breath, could bring the universe into existence, then His ability to breathe His Holy Word into the writers of scripture without error is both logical and believable.

The process of illumination involves the Holy Spirit helping individuals understand the truth of God's Word. In essence, the Holy Spirit enlightens the heart. (Psalm 119:130, NLT) declares, *"The teaching of your word gives light, so even the simple can understand."* Illumination is like a light breaking through the darkness, bringing enlightenment and understanding. (Psalm 119:18, NKJV) says, *"Open my eyes* **(that's illumination)** *that I may see* **(see what?)** *wonderful things* **(from where?)** *in your law."* **(His Word)** Regular study and meditation on God's Word bring direction and discernment, helping believers navigate the complexities of life.

As we walk in faith and are led by the Spirit, let us declare our unwavering trust in God's Word, echoing the sentiments of the Psalmist: *"Your eternal word, O LORD, stands firm in heaven. Your faithfulness extends to every generation, as enduring as the earth you created. Your regulations remain true to this day, for everything serves your plans"* (Psalm 119:89-91, NLT).

In the words of Martin Luther, *"To hear or to read the scriptures is nothing less than to hear from God."* The Bible, with its unmatched influence, remains a beacon of truth and a timeless guide. Trusting the Word of God is not just an act of faith; it is anchoring our lives in the unwavering promises of the Almighty.

As we journey through the pages of scripture in the days ahead, may we approach God's Word with reverence, anticipation, and a deep trust in its life-transforming power.

I'll conclude with a reminder that the Bible is the most translated, the most published, the most quoted, and the most influential book in the history of mankind. It's true today, it will be true tomorrow, and it will be true forever and ever; Amen.

> *"Heavenly Father, my deep desire is to be fully confident in your holy Word. May the revelation of Your Word, the inspiration of Your Word, and the illumination of Your Word encourage and strengthen my faith so I will be anchored in Your promises and truth, Amen."*

DAY 63

Empty Tomb or Empty Faith

Read: 1 Corinthians 15:50-58

The empty tomb is not merely a historical event; it's the foundation of our faith, and the cornerstone of the gospel. Without the resurrection, our faith would be empty—void of life, hope, and eternal significance. The empty tomb challenges scepticism, provides answers, and proclaims a timeless truth that continues to transform lives today.

In 1 Corinthians 15, Paul passionately defends the resurrection, presenting compelling arguments to counter scepticism. In verse 12 (NLT), he poses a question, *"But tell me this—since we preach that Christ rose from the dead, why are some of you saying there will be no resurrection of the dead?"* Maybe his question was rhetorical because in the following verse, he tells the Corinthians that if there is no resurrection of the dead, then not even Christ has been raised. (v13) His defence goes on to point out in verses 14-18 that if this is the case, then our preaching is in vain and our faith is in vain, making believers false witnesses, leaving our faith worthless. However, Christianity stands on the truth that Christ has conquered death, securing eternal life for all believers.

Moving to the explanation of the resurrection, Paul addresses questions from doubters. Using powerful imagery, he illustrates how our earthly bodies, like seeds planted in the ground, undergo a transformation. Did you know that each cell of the wheat plant signals the plant's own impending death? New life depends on replanting the seeds it produces. The seeds become places where new life begins again. The seeds must first be separated from life. The plant must die and be lifeless before it can become of any use. If you want to start a new plant, you must tear the living plant out and then plant the seeds. Or, you can just let the seeds drop and hope they will reproduce by themselves. People call this nature, but really, this is God's wonderfully designed creation at its best. In the context of replanting, Paul emphasizes that believers, united with Christ in His death and resurrection, will receive new bodies—spiritual bodies that mirror Christ's resurrection. This transformation hinges on the spiritual seed planted within us, received by dying to ourselves and being born again. A powerful picture, isn't it?

Paul then transitions again to the proclamation of the resurrection, unveiling the transfiguring power of this event. Believers are urged to put aside their earthly bodies, anticipating a glorious transformation. This transformation, whether experienced during the believer's life or after their death, is a mystery—a divine process beyond complete human comprehension. What we know for sure is that the resurrection will occur with the last trumpet blast, delivering believers from the clutches of death in the blink of an eye.

The Lord's second coming or advent should prompt believers like you and me to live with purpose, recognizing that our labour for the Lord will never be in vain. Paul's exhortation in this passage echoes through time, urging all Christians to engage in abundant works for the Lord. As we await the resurrection, we are to invest in heavenly treasures, understanding that our efforts will be worth it. In the waiting, may we be reminded that the resurrection is not just a future event; it must shape our present, and give purpose and meaning to our lives as we eagerly await the glorious day when we will be transformed.

As this devotion concludes, Paul highlights the believer's calling in light of the impending resurrection. Until Christ's return, believers are called to be steadfast, immovable, and to abound in the work of the Lord.

Steadfastness requires a constant walk with God and the Holy Spirit, immovability calls for unwavering focus despite life's challenges, and abounding in the Lord's work demands investing in heavenly treasures.

189

"Lord, today as I contemplate your return and the resurrection, may my faith be vibrant, my hope unwavering, and my life abound in the work of the Lord, all for your glory and honour, Amen."

DAY 64

STAYING CONNECTED TO THE VINE

Read: John 15:1-13

In Matthew chapters 5–7, Jesus taught His followers what life in God's kingdom looks like. In the Sermon on the Mount, He spoke about being salt and light, dealing with anger and lust, loving our enemies, praying sincerely, handling money wisely, resisting worry, and avoiding judgmental hearts. Then, as He came to the close of that teaching, Jesus addressed an even deeper issue—what it truly means to be His disciple.

Jesus warned His listeners that not everyone who claims to follow Him actually belongs to Him. He said we would recognize true disciples not by their words, but by their fruit. Good trees bear good fruit, and bad trees do not. The message is clear: authentic faith produces visible evidence. But that leads us to an important question—how do we produce fruit that pleases God?

Jesus answers that question clearly in (John 15:1-2, NLT) when he said, "*I am the true grapevine, and my Father is the gardener. He cuts off every branch of mine that doesn't produce fruit, and he prunes the branches that do bear fruit so they will produce even more."* In this picture, Jesus is the vine, the Father is the gardener, and we are the branches. Life, nourishment, and fruitfulness all flow from one source—our connection to Christ.

Many people followed Jesus during His earthly ministry, but not all were true believers. Some followed Him out of curiosity. Others were drawn by the miracles or the excitement of the crowds. Even among the twelve disciples, Judas appeared connected for a time. Yet, his life revealed that he was not truly abiding in Christ. He was cut off, while the remaining disciples were lovingly pruned so they could become more fruitful.

Jesus makes it unmistakably clear that bearing fruit is impossible apart from Him. He says in (John 15:4–5, NLT), *"Remain in me, and I will remain in you. For a branch cannot produce fruit if it is severed from the vine… Yes, I am the vine; you are the branches. Those who remain in me… will produce much fruit. For apart from me you can do nothing."* The word remain is the heartbeat of this passage, and to remain in Christ means to trust Him, obey Him, persevere in faith, and live daily in dependence on Him.

I am reminded of a grapevine that grew beside a shed at the first home we purchased. Every spring, healthy branches showed clear signs of life—they were flexible, green, and growing. But the dead branches were brittle and lifeless. They produced nothing and only cluttered the vine. The gardener's job was simple: remove what was dead and prune what was living so that good fruit could grow. In the same way, God lovingly removes what hinders growth and prunes our lives so we can bear fruit that brings Him glory. Unless you have seen it with your own eyes, you wouldn't believe how much more fruit our grapevine produced after we removed the dead vine branches.

Jesus explains that remaining in Him is inseparable from remaining in His love. In (John 15:9–10, NLT), He says, *"I have loved you even as the Father has loved me. Remain in my love. When you obey my commandments, you remain in my love."* Obedience is not a burden—it's the pathway to intimacy with Christ. When we walk in loving obedience, we stay connected to the vine.

Now, one result of this connection is joy. Jesus says in (John 15:11, NLT), *"I have told you these things so that you will be filled with my joy. Yes, your joy will overflow!"* Joy is not produced by circumstances; it flows from communion with Christ. When we remain in Him, His joy becomes our strength.

Remaining in the vine also leads to loving others. Jesus concludes this passage by reminding us that the greatest expression of love is sacrifice. "*There is no greater love than to lay down one's life for one's friends*" (John 15:13, NLT). A life connected to Christ will be marked by a sacrificial love for fellow believers and compassion for the lost.

To stay connected to the vine means choosing obedience, prayer, devotion to God's Word, and a self-giving love that reflects Christ. When we do, spiritual fruit will grow, God will be glorified, and our lives will testify that we truly belong to Him.

> *"Dear Lord, I want to thank You for sending Jesus, the true Vine, who gives me life and hope. I confess that there are times when I try to live in my own strength instead of remaining fully connected to Him. Teach me to abide in Christ daily—to trust, obey, and walk closely with Him and help my life bear fruit that will reflect Jesus to others. In His precious name, Amen."*

THE LOST ART OF COMMITMENT
(CALLING ALL MEN)

Read: Joshua 24:11-15

We live in a time when commitment seems like a lost art, especially among men. It's hard to deny that there's a noticeable absence of steadfast leadership in our homes, marriages, parenting, and, sadly, in our churches. The prevailing mindset has shifted from enduring commitments to transient experiences, as exemplified by the declining duration of marriages. Today's relationships often hinge on feelings rather than enduring commitments, resulting in an average marriage span of approximately eight years. Oh, how this must grieve God because this trend leaves many children growing up without the consistent presence of a father figure.

The biblical injunction for husbands to love their wives as Christ loves the church underscores the importance of commitment in family life. Yet, present-day marriages frequently prioritize personal feelings over commitment, leading to a myriad of challenges. This deficiency in commitment extends beyond the family unit, impacting the health and vitality of our churches.

The call to reestablish the lost art of commitment is a challenge to men and all Christians to reassess their priorities and embrace a more committed lifestyle. But this transformation will require prayerful self-examination and bold life changes.

Reflecting on our passage today, we witness Joshua's poignant plea to the Israelites. In this assembly, Joshua reiterates the victories God granted them, urging the people to remain committed to the Lord. As Joshua's life and leadership approach their conclusion, he presents a challenge and charge to persevere in commitment to God even after his departure. The central theme revolves around the people's choice of commitment.

We read today that Joshua gathered the tribes at Shechem. He summoned the elders, leaders, judges, and officers. He challenged them to choose whom they will serve. This narrative contains a profound life application, urging all to fear the Lord and serve Him wholeheartedly. Joshua, in no uncertain terms, declared his unwavering commitment: *"As for me and my family, we will serve the Lord"* (Joshua 24:15 NLT).

Today's world reflects what we see in the Bible. Long-term commitments are often set aside in favour of short-term experiences. An examination of our churches reveals a decline, with many congregations dwindling or closing their doors altogether. This phenomenon often results from a reluctance or outright refusal to commit fully to God.

Joshua's exhortation to destroy ancestral idols is a symbolic call to eliminate distractions that will hinder our commitment to Christ and his Church. Today, these distractions manifest as the idols of time, money, talents, and personal desires. We must all remember that anything prioritized above God constitutes an idol and will divert our focus from our divine commitments.

Joshua's charge here is to serve the Lord alone, underscoring the need to eliminate idols that threaten our commitment. This call resonates with urgency, urging Christ's disciples to lead and serve God's purpose. As we witness the absence of male leadership across various church roles, there must be a renewed call for men to fill these essential roles.

A notable illustration underscores the dedication of women within the church, as they lead committees, ministries, and initiatives. While we appreciate their commitment, we urge men today to step forward, embrace leadership, and serve God wholeheartedly.

In a generation where commitment waivers, the call to be men of faith, men of God, and men of courage resonates profoundly. Like Joshua, who stood firm in his commitment even in his final moments, the charge is to give up our will for His will. It is a challenge to daily deny ourselves, take up our cross, and follow Jesus.

The concluding call is for contemporary men to turn the ship around and lead with commitment, reestablishing the lost art of commitment. The commitment to fear the Lord, to serve Him wholeheartedly, and to put away idols is crucial. A plea is extended to confidently declare, *"As for me and my household, we will serve the Lord."* May this cry resonate throughout our congregations, leading to a renewed commitment in our homes, churches, and lives.

> *"Lord, I pray that as a church, your bride, we will have a renewed sense of commitment. I pray that both men and women will stand up and surrender to you daily, and serve you with all their heart so that you will be glorified, Amen."*

PROCLAIMING FREEDOM

Read: Isaiah 61:1-7

I read a story about a lawyer who was driving his new BMW on a mountain road in the middle of a snowstorm. Losing control, the car veers toward the cliff. The driver scrambles to exit the car. In the process, his arm was caught and was torn off as his new BMW went over the cliff and up in flames. A truck driver following him stopped to help. He saw that the man had lost his arm and said we should look for it, but the man looked where his arm had been and said, "Oh no, my Rolex!" This amusing story serves as a stark reminder of the transient nature of worldly pursuits and possessions, echoing the timeless wisdom of Jesus in Mark 8:36 (NLT): "And how do you benefit if you gain the whole world but lose your own soul in the process?"

In the story of the prodigal son found in Luke chapter 15, the son grapples with priorities and poor choices. Struggling amidst financial ruin and humbled in the dust, the prodigal son stands at a crossroads.

This story masterfully interlaces themes of Healing, Hope, and Second Chances, which is the subtitle of my debut novel, "*Up From the Ashes.*" The father in the parable embodies forgiveness, mercy, and grace, echoing the profound restoration foretold in Isaiah's prophecy.

Isaiah, who wrote today's passage, is known as the *„evangelical prophet" and offers* prophetic insights into the Messiah's character and ministry. In this passage, Isaiah speaks directly about the Messiah, His Ministry, and Our Mission.

The Messiah, identified as Jesus, steps into the spotlight as the prophesied Redeemer. A journey through Luke 4:18-19 reveals Jesus claiming the fulfilment of Isaiah 61:1, a proclamation that is met with anger, reflecting the divisive claims of His divinity found elsewhere in the Gospels.

Transitioning to the Messiah's Ministry, we see in verse one that Jesus came to share the good news to the poor and to set the captives free. He makes this possible by proclaiming that he will be the sacrificial Lamb of God that will reconcile people to God. John 3:16 and Romans 10:9-10 illuminate the profound truth that Jesus' death and resurrection pave the way to eternal life.

Those who are set free from the bondage of sin are urged to recognize their ongoing need for Christ, as John 15:5 illustrates: apart from God, believers can do nothing.

The application of today's devotional is Our Mission, as portrayed in Isaiah 61:6, depicting believers as *"priests of the Lord"* and *"ministers of our God."* This special designation conveys a unique relationship with God and a call to devoted service.

When the true believer fully comprehends who the Messiah is and what he has done to set them free, they will faithfully embrace their mission, knowing that, as in Isaiah 61:6-7, God rewards His servants with honour and everlasting joy.

Today's devotional reminds us that Jesus came to proclaim true freedom. This freedom reaches beyond the present moment and into eternity. This good news calls us, as His followers, to lift our eyes above what is temporary and to live for what truly lasts. As you walk with Christ and are led by the Spirit, let me ask you this question. Are you embracing the mission He has given you—a mission that brings glory to God and leads to lasting joy in His presence? If your answer is no or you are unsure, tomorrow's devotional will address how you and I can plant the seed of faith.

> *"Lord, I know the prophesied Messiah came to set people free from their sins and that he invites his followers to minister to him and for him by sharing the good news of Jesus Christ. My prayer is that as the Lord provides opportunities to be his hands and feet, that I will be faithful in sharing my faith with others so they too can taste and see that the Lord is good, Amen."*

PLANTING THE SEED OF FAITH

Read: Exodus 2:1-9

On our journey of faith, God calls us to be sowers—people who faithfully scatter seeds of truth, hope, and then trust in Him to bring a harvest. Now, whether in our homes, workplaces, churches, or communities, our daily lives present countless opportunities to plant seeds of faith. While we may never fully see the outcome of our efforts, we are invited to trust God to bring about a harvest in His perfect timing.

In Exodus 2:1–9, we encounter a powerful example of seed-planting faith in the life of Moses' mother, Jochebed. Living under Pharaoh's brutal decree that all Hebrew baby boys were to be killed, she faced unimaginable fear and uncertainty. Yet Scripture tells us, *"Now a man of the tribe of Levi married a Levite woman, and she became pregnant and gave birth to a son. When she saw that he was a fine child, she hid him for three months"* (Exodus 2:1–2 NIV). Her actions reveal a woman who trusted God more than she feared the king.

When she could no longer hide her son, Jochebed took a courageous step of faith. "*She got a papyrus basket for him and coated it with tar and pitch. Then she placed the child in it and put it among the reeds along the bank of the Nile*" (Exodus 2:3 NIV). Rather than surrendering her son to despair, she entrusted him to God. This was not an act of abandonment, but of belief. She planted a seed of faith—placing Moses in God's hands and trusting Him to do what she could not.

Like Moses' mother, we are called to prepare the soil for God's work in the lives of those around us. Farmers know that seeds cannot grow unless the ground is properly cultivated. Scripture echoes this truth: "*Sow righteousness for yourselves, reap the fruit of unfailing love, and break up your unplowed ground; for it is time to seek the Lord*" (Hosea 10:12, NIV). Before we can influence others, our own hearts must be soft, surrendered, and aligned with God's will.

As we plant seeds of faith, we must also be intentional about what we sow. The apostle Paul instructs believers, "*Whatever is true, whatever is noble, whatever is right, whatever is pure, whatever is lovely, whatever is admirable—if anything is excellent or praiseworthy—think about such things*" (Philippians 4:8, NIV). Our words, attitudes, and actions shape the seeds we scatter. Whether through teaching, mentoring, or simply living out our faith authentically, we have the opportunity to pass on God's truth to the next generation.

Planting, however, is only part of the process. Seeds must also be nurtured. Growth requires care, patience, and community. The writer of Hebrews reminds us, "*Let us hold unswervingly to the hope we profess, for he who promised is faithful. And let us consider how we may spur one another on toward love and good deeds*" (Hebrews 10:23–24 NIV). God often uses fellowship, encouragement, and accountability within the body of Christ to water the seeds that have been planted.

Finally, we must learn to trust God with the harvest. Jochebed did not live to see all that God would accomplish through Moses. Yet, her obedience played a vital role in God's redemptive plan. Scripture reassures us, "*Start children off on the way they should go, and even when they are old they will not turn from it*" (Proverbs 22:6, NIV). While we may not always witness the fruit of our labour, God promises that faithful sowing is never wasted.

As we reflect on the faith of Moses' mother and the quiet work of planting seeds, we are reminded that God calls us to live with purpose and trust. Though it is the Lord alone who brings the growth, He graciously invites you and me to take part in His work. May we sow our seeds faithfully, care for them diligently, and wait with patient hearts—confident that our labour in the Lord will bear fruit in His perfect time.

"Lord, as I reflect on the faith of Moses' mother, I am reminded that You call Your people not only to plant seeds of faith, but also to water and nurture them. Help me to be faithful in sowing truth, love, and obedience into the lives of those around me. In the name of Jesus, I pray, Amen."

DAY 68

EXPERIENCING UNSPEAKABLE JOY

Read: 1 Peter 1:3-9

The message of Christ's birth is one of profound joy. From the angelic announcement of His arrival to the empty tomb and the promise of His return, joy weaves its way through every part of the Christian faith. Scripture repeatedly calls God's people to rejoice, reminding us that the coming of Christ brought glad tidings to all the world. Yet, despite this unchanging truth, many believers struggle to experience joy in their daily lives. Joy often feels elusive, especially in seasons of hardship or uncertainty. To understand how we can experience unspeakable joy, we must rediscover its true source.

Peter begins his letter with a powerful declaration: *"Blessed be the God and Father of our Lord Jesus Christ, who according to His abundant mercy has begotten us again to a living hope through the resurrection of Jesus Christ from the dead"* (1 Peter 1:3 NLT). Our joy is rooted in what God has done for us through Christ. It is not a shallow happiness dependent on our circumstances, but a deep, spiritual reality anchored in God's mercy and grace.

Christians find true joy in the reality of Christ's birth. The angel told Zechariah concerning John the Baptist, *"And you will have joy and gladness, and many will rejoice at his birth"* (Luke 1:14 NLT). Later, the angel announced to the shepherds, *"Do not be afraid, for behold, I bring you good tidings of great joy which will be to all people"* (Luke 2:10 NLT). The birth of Jesus was not merely a historical event—it was God stepping into human history to redeem His creation.

Our joy flows not just from Christ's arrival, but from His mission. Jesus came to reconcile sinful people to a holy God. Knowing that God loved us enough to send His Son should fill our hearts with gratitude and wonder. This truth alone is more than enough reason to rejoice, regardless of what we face.

Beyond Christ's birth, our joy is anchored in the assurance of eternal salvation. Peter reminds believers that we have *"an inheritance incorruptible and undefiled and that does not fade away, reserved in heaven for you"* (1 Peter 1:4 NLT). Earthly treasures will fade, but our heavenly inheritance is secure and will endure for all eternity.

Jesus Himself taught that joy is possible even in suffering: *"Blessed are you when men hate you... Rejoice in that day and leap for joy! For indeed your reward is great in heaven"* (Luke 6:22–23 NLT). Having this perspective enables us to endure trials with hope. Peter acknowledges that believers may be *"grieved by various trials"* (1 Peter 1:6 NLT), yet those trials refine our faith and lead to praise and glory when Christ is revealed.

While joy is a gift from God, it's also a daily choice. Paul commands believers, *"Rejoice in the Lord always. Again I will say, rejoice!"* (Philippians 4:4 NLT). This instruction assumes that joy is not automatic. Choosing joy means deliberately focusing on God's faithfulness rather than our difficulties.

It's important to note that our joy needs to be a testimony to the world in times of difficulty. When believers rejoice in the midst of hardship, it demonstrates the transforming power of Christ at work within them. This kind of joy cannot be explained by human logic and is evidence of a living faith within us.

Also, remember that true joy is not found in success or possessions. Jesus said, *"These things I have spoken to you, that My joy may remain in you, and that your joy may be full*" (John 15:11 NLT). Joy flows from abiding in Christ. Anything else will only offer temporary satisfaction.

The psalmist declares, "*You will show me the path of life; In Your presence is fullness of joy*" (Psalm 16:11 NLT). As we draw near to God through prayer, worship, and His Word, we will experience a joy that transcends our own understanding. This type of joy will sustain us, strengthen us, and remind us that we belong to Him.

Peter beautifully describes this joy as a "*joy inexpressible and full of glory*" (1 Peter 1:8 NLT). It is joy that words cannot fully capture—a joy grounded in faith, fuelled by hope, and secured by salvation. This is the difference between happiness and joy. Happiness depends on what happens to us, and joy depends on who holds us.

You and I don't have to wait until the next Advent season to celebrate the unspeakable joy He offers. We need to rejoice in the Lord every day so that our lives will reflect the joy of our salvation, which, in turn, will draw others to our loving Saviour.

> "*Heavenly Father, I thank You for the unspeakable joy that comes through faith in Jesus Christ. I confess that there are times when I allow circumstances to steal my joy. Help me to keep my eyes fixed on the living hope I have in Christ and the eternal inheritance You have promised, and may the joy of my salvation be evident in my life and bring glory to You. In Christ's name I pray, Amen.*"

SALT AND LIGHT

Read: Matthew 5:13-16

As believers, we are familiar with Jesus' profound declaration that we are the "Salt and Light" of the world. Yet, what does this truly mean, and why did Jesus choose this phrase to describe His followers?

The concept of Christians being the salt of the earth and the light of the world is a powerful illustration of our influence and visibility in society. Let's explore each of these roles individually, beginning with:

The Salt of the World

Salt symbolizes our Christian influence. Just as salt enhances the flavour of food and preserves it, our influence should season and preserve the world around us. However, like salt, our impact must be balanced; too little, and it goes unnoticed, too much, and it can be overwhelming.

Throughout history, salt was highly prized for its seasoning and preservative qualities, even serving as a form of currency. It made food palatable and was a symbol of covenant relationships. Similarly, as the salt of the earth, we are called to flavour the lives of those around us with the principles of God's kingdom.

It has been nicely said that, "*Jesus, looking out over the multitudes of His day, saw the corruption, the disintegration of life at every point, its breakup, its spoliation; and because of His love of the multitudes, He knew the thing that they needed most was the salt in order that the corruption should be arrested.*" G.C. Campbell Morgan

Jesus's injunction to be salt implies a silent but potent witness. Our influence should permeate society, bringing about positive change and pointing others towards the kingdom of God. Just as salt changes the taste of food, our presence should transform the communities we inhabit.

The Light of the World

Likewise, Jesus refers to His followers as the light of the world, signifying our testimony and visibility. Light exposes darkness, serves as a guide, and must be seen to fulfill its purpose. We are the reflection of the true light, Jesus Christ, who illuminates the path for others to follow.

A simple yet important truth about light is that light exposes darkness, serves as a guide, and needs to be seen.

Just as Jesus proclaimed Himself as the light of the world, we too must reflect His light in our lives. Through our actions, words, and deeds, we reveal the character of God to those around us. Our lives should serve as beacons of hope and truth in a world overshadowed by fear and uncertainty, as we see all around us today.

As reflectors of the light, our task is to shine brightly, guiding others towards the source of light and life, Jesus Christ. We expose the darkness, provide direction, and draw people into the warmth of God's love.

We must remember that no one lights a light only to put it under a basket or earthen vessel, and one small candle can cast light into a dark room.

To fulfil our calling as the salt and light of the world, we must actively engage with society, showing genuine love and compassion to those around us. Just as salt loses its effectiveness when confined to the shaker, our influence diminishes when we isolate ourselves from the world.

We are called to be both the seasoning that flavours and the light that dispels darkness. Our interactions should reflect the love of Christ, drawing others into a relationship with Him. Whether through ministries or in our day-to-day life, we have the opportunity to impact lives and spread the message of God's grace.

As we continue on our journey, let's embrace our identity as the salt and light of the world. The Apostle Paul said, *"For God, who said, 'let light shine out of darkness,' made his light shine in our hearts to give us the light of the knowledge of God's glory displayed in the face of Christ."* (2 Corinthians 4:6 NIV) With this truth, may our lives reflect the love and truth of Jesus Christ and bring hope to those in need. Together, let us shine brightly for the glory of God in our communities and beyond.

> *"Father, I want my faith to be seen by others as 'salt and light.' I desire to season and preserve the lives of those around me, and I want your light to shine through me. You have brought me out of darkness into your wonderful light, and I want my light to shine before others so you will receive the honour and glory. Amen"*

The Power of Prayer

Read: James 5:13-16

Life can be unpredictable, can't it? Sometimes, it feels like we're sailing along smoothly, and then, out of nowhere, a storm hits. While serving as a pastor in a small town, there was a week when our community experienced just that. We saw the raw power of nature, the destruction it could unleash, and the disruption it caused in our everyday lives. Trees down, power out for days, and homes damaged. It was a stark reminder that bad things happen, even to good people.

Our own family wasn't spared. Our boat sustained damage, and then, as if that wasn't enough, my wife's car started smoking downtown. Even our Vacation Bible School got off to a rocky start, missing its first two nights. In a world impacted by sin, these kinds of challenges are simply a reality we face.

When these difficult moments arise, what's our first response? It's so easy to fall into worry, isn't it? We fret about what's lost, what might happen next, and how we'll possibly navigate the mess. But the Bible offers us a different, and far more powerful, approach. (Philippians 4:6 NLT) gives us this incredible instruction: *«Don't worry about anything; instead, pray about everything. Tell God what you need, and thank him for all he has done."*

This verse is more than just a nice suggestion; it's a blueprint for living. It tells us to replace our anxiety with prayer. And why should we pray instead of worry? Because, as we're going to explore today, there is incredible power in prayer.

In our passage today, the Apostle James offers profound wisdom on how to respond to life's various circumstances. He begins by addressing different situations we will all find ourselves in at some point. He asks three important questions and provides the answers to them:

- Are any of you suffering hardships? You should pray.
- Are any of you happy? You should sing praises.
- Are any of you sick? You should call for the elders of the church to come and pray over you, anointing you with oil in the name of the Lord.

Here, James lays out a clear path for us. When we're struggling, we are instructed and encouraged to pray. When we're experiencing joy, we are to offer praise. And when we are sick, there are specific steps outlined for us within the church family.

Our focus today is on the instructions for those who are sick. We will all get sick from time to time, and some will become seriously ill. When this happens, James tells us they should *"call for the elders of the church to come and pray over you, anointing you with oil in the name of the Lord."* This is a powerful directive that highlights the importance of community and faith in times of illness.

Notice the first instruction: *"Call for the elders."* It's a simple yet significant command. Sometimes, when we're sick or facing a difficult time, we might hesitate to reach out; that's our human nature. Maybe, we might think we're a burden, or that church leaders are too busy. Please, let me assure you that it is not the case. For elders, it's part of their calling to be there for you, to pray with you and for you. So please, don't ever feel like you can't reach out.

The second instruction is to *"pray over you."* This simply means praying for you. James shows us different kinds of prayer throughout this passage: praying for ourselves when we're in trouble, praying for the sick, and praying for each other. Life is unpredictable, full of triumphs and tragedies, joy and sorrow, health and sickness. In all these seasons, prayer is our lifeline.

(Psalm 34:4 NLT) reminds us of the power of prayer in times of fear and trouble: *"I prayed to the LORD, and he answered me. He freed me from all my fears."* When life feels like it's falling apart, we can pray for wisdom, for strength, and for God's will to be done. We have the incredible privilege, through Jesus, to approach our heavenly Father anytime, anywhere, with anything on our hearts.

The third instruction for the sick is to be *"anointed with oil."* This can sometimes be a confusing part of the passage, but let's keep it simple. Does God answer prayer? Yes! Does He answer prayer for the sick? Yes! Does He sometimes answer in ways that seem miraculous? Yes! Does He always answer according to His perfect will? Yes!

These are foundational truths. God can do infinitely more than we can ask or imagine, as Ephesians 3:20 reminds us. The act of anointing with oil, often olive oil, has historical significance. The Bible mentions olive oil numerous times, and it was recognized for its medicinal properties. While the oil itself doesn't heal, it serves as a powerful symbol of healing, health, and vitality.

James emphasizes that the healing comes from God, not the oil. He says in verse 16, *"The earnest prayer of a righteous person has great power and produces wonderful results."* The power is in the prayer offered in faith, and in the name of the Lord.

Whether healing comes quickly or slowly, through a miracle, medicine, or a combination of both, the truth remains: God can heal His children. And in our passage today, one of the roles of Church leaders is to come to the sick, to pray for them when they ask, and to anoint them with oil as a symbol of that potential healing. Jesus is the Great Physician, and it is in His name that we pray and anoint.

> *"Lord, when the storms of life hit, let my first response be prayer. I pray that I will not succumb to worry, but instead, that I will turn my heart and my voice to the one who holds my tomorrows. Thank you for reminding me that there is indeed great power in prayer, and it can produce wonderful results in my life, Amen."*

DAY 71

STANDING ON THE PROMISES OF GOD

Read: Galatians 3:15-29

How are you at keeping promises? In a society where commitments are often broken, it's a common struggle. Personally, over the years, I've broken promises to my wife, my children, my co-workers, and my bosses. However, since becoming a Christian, I've made a conscious effort not to break my promises, but I still do sometimes.

Consider the story of Bill, a devout Christian who worked in retail but was offered a position in Youth Ministry at his church. He promised his job to a non-Christian friend named Tim, whom he had been witnessing to. When faced with the possibility that the church position might not work out, Bill kept his promise, honouring his word and maintaining his integrity.

What would you have done in this situation? Would you think twice about keeping your promise if circumstances changed? In Psalm 15:4, David tells us that God honours those who keep their promises, even when it's difficult.

As Christians, we strive to keep our promises because we follow a God who makes and keeps promises. The hymn *"Standing on the Promises of God"* echoes this commitment, reminding us of the foundation on which we stand.

Now, let's look more closely into Galatians 3:15-29 to explore the promises of God. Paul begins by giving an everyday example in verse 15, emphasizing the irrevocable nature of agreements. He draws parallels to God's promises to Abraham, stressing that they remain unbroken. This sets the stage for understanding the relationship between God's law and His promises.

In verse 19, Paul addresses the question: *"Why was the law given?"* The law, given through Moses, served a specific purpose. It pointed out our sins and revealed our need for a Saviour. It was never intended to contradict God's promises but to complement them.

The new covenant promised in Jeremiah 31:31-34 finds fulfilment in Jesus Christ. This covenant offers a personal relationship with God, with His laws written on our hearts. It's through Christ's blood that this promise becomes a reality.

Paul strongly denies any conflict between God's law and His promises. Instead, he asserts that the law reveals our need for salvation and that salvation is attainable only through faith in Jesus Christ.

The law served as a guardian until Christ's arrival, guiding us to recognize our need for salvation. In verses 26-27, Paul declares that, through faith in Christ, we become children of God and are united with Him in baptism. There is no longer any distinction based on nationality, social status, or gender. All are one in Christ Jesus.

Closing with verse 29, Paul assures us that, belonging to Christ, we are true children of Abraham and heirs to the promises God gave him.

As we navigate life, let's remember and stand on the following promises of God:

- **His Presence:** God promises to be with us always. (Matthew 28:20)
- **His Power:** We have permission to approach Him with confidence. (Hebrews 4:16)
- **His Provision:** He ensures our needs are met. (Philippians 4:19)

- **Our Place in Heaven:** Our eternal home is secure. (John 14:2-3)
- **His Peace, Grace, Goodness:** God provides these abundantly. (John 14:27)
- **His Faithfulness and Forgiveness:** God is unwavering in His love. (1 John 1:9)
- **His Strength:** In times of weakness, He sustains us. (Isaiah 40:29)
- **Our Saviour and the Holy Spirit:** We are never alone. (Matthew 1:21)
- **A Heart for the Broken:** God's compassion flows through us. (Psalm 34:18)
- **Courage, Character, Compassion:** These virtues are His gifts. (Joshua 1:9)

Whether we are on the mountain or in the deepest valley, we can count on these promises to be the foundation of our lives. So, let's boldly declare, *"I'm standing on the promises of God!"*

> *"Lord, I want to stand on Your promises every day. Please, by the power of the Holy Spirit, may I be reminded of them every morning when I wake up. In Jesus mighty name I pray, Amen."*

REAL LOVE

Read: 1 John 4:20-5:5

Everyone is searching for real love. We hear about it in songs, see it in movies, and read about it in books — yet many still wonder what it truly is and where it can be found. Jesus made it clear: real love begins with loving God and then loving others. In (Matthew 22:37–39 NLT), He said, "You must love the Lord your God with all your heart, all your soul, and all your mind... and love your neighbour as yourself."

It sounds simple, but it isn't easy, especially in a world where love is often defined by emotion or convenience. We must remember that Jesus calls us to a love that is deeper, purer, and lasting — a love that reflects the heart of God Himself.

Real love transforms lives and isn't based on feelings but on action. It's not measured by what we say but by how we live. John wrote, "*If someone says, 'I love God,' but hates a fellow believer, that person is a liar; for if we don't love people we can see, how can we love God, whom we cannot see?"* (1 John 4:20 NLT). Our love for God is proven by our love for others, especially when it's hard.

To experience real love, today's scripture gives us three vital principles: Be Honest, Be Obedient, and Be Victorious.

1. Be Honest

John reminds us that we cannot claim to love God while holding onto bitterness or resentment toward others. Real love begins when we are honest with God, with ourselves, and with those around us.

Honesty is a sign of spiritual maturity. It means admitting when we've fallen short, seeking forgiveness, and taking steps to make things right. Pretending may have been part of childhood play, but spiritual pretending keeps us from growing in Christ. God desires truth from the inside out. He delights in hearts that are sincere and transparent before Him.

When we walk in honesty, we walk in freedom. We stop pretending, start healing, and begin reflecting the genuine love of Christ to the world around us.

2. Be Obedient

John continues, *"We know we love God's children if we love God and obey his commandments. Loving God means keeping his commandments, and his commandments are not burdensome."* (1 John 5:2–3 NLT).

True love for God always produces obedience. When our hearts are aligned with His will, obedience no longer feels heavy — it becomes a joy. We obey not out of fear, but out of love.

Even creation obeys the Creator. The wind and waves respond to His word; the stars stay in place because He commands them to. Shouldn't we, as His children, joyfully follow His lead?

Another important note: God doesn't want half-hearted obedience. He desires surrendered hearts that delight in doing His will. Just as Paul reminded the Corinthians that *"God loves a person who gives cheerfully"* (2 Corinthians 9:7 NLT), He also loves a believer who obeys cheerfully out of gratitude, not obligation.

3. Be Victorious

Finally, John declares, *"For every child of God defeats this evil world, and we achieve this victory through our faith."* (1 John 5:4 NLT).

When we live honestly and obediently before God, we walk in victory. This victory isn't about escaping problems but overcoming them through faith in Christ. The same power that raised Jesus from the dead lives within every believer. Through Him, we are conquerors — not because of our strength, but because of His.

Faith and love grow together. The more we love Christ, the more we trust Him; and the more we trust Him, the stronger our faith becomes. When love matures, faith deepens, and that's where real victory is found.

So, if you're searching for real love, look no further than Jesus Christ. He is love in its purest form. Be honest with Him about where you are. Choose obedience, not out of duty but out of devotion. And walk in the victory that comes through faith — knowing that nothing can separate you from His love.

> *"Father, thank You for showing me what real love looks like through Your Son, Jesus Christ. Teach me to love honestly, obey joyfully, and walk victoriously in faith. Help me love others the way You have loved me — unconditionally and sacrificially. When my love grows weak, strengthen me by Your Spirit so that my life reflects Your heart. In Jesus' mighty name I pray, Amen."*

DAY 73

Are You Being a True Neighbour?

Read: Luke 10:25-37

Do you ever struggle with doing God's will? You read a verse or hear a sermon and know exactly what God wants you to do, yet you wrestle with it? Well, you're not alone—I've been there too.

If you had told me years ago that I'd one day be preaching and the Pastor of a church, I would have said, "You're crazy." I wasn't a public speaker, and I didn't have the voice for it. When I felt called to serve as a Pastor, I even told God, "I can't do this." But He saw things differently. Like Moses, who told God he wasn't good with words, I discovered that when we're willing, God will equip us to complete the task He has for us.

That same truth applies to loving our neighbours. God doesn't ask us to do it because it's easy; He calls us to love others because it reflects His heart.

When Jesus told the parable of the Good Samaritan, He answered the question, *"Who is my neighbour?"* not with a definition, but with a demonstration. The Samaritan didn't just talk about love—he lived it. He crossed cultural and personal barriers to care for someone in need. And Jesus says, *"Go and do the same."*

I remember being convicted about this very thing when my wife and I moved into a new neighbourhood. After two months, I realized we hadn't yet introduced ourselves to our neighbours, and it bothered me. So, I sat down and wrote a handwritten letter to each household on our street, introducing our family and expressing that we looked forward to getting to know them. My daughter Brittany delivered them to each mailbox, and before long, one neighbour called to thank us. Another wrote us back. Small gestures opened doors for connection. I learned something that day—if you want to touch your neighbours, you must first be willing to reach out.

Loving our neighbour doesn't always look grand or dramatic. Sometimes it's a handwritten note, a plate of cookies, or a listening ear. But those small acts, done in Jesus' name, carry eternal weight.

The Bible emphasizes this truth again and again. Jesus said, *"Love your neighbour as yourself"* (Matthew 22:39 NLT). Paul wrote that all the commandments can be summed up in this one command (Romans 13:9), and James called it *"the royal law"* (James 2:8). God takes this command seriously—and so should we.

Loving your neighbour means more than being kind to people you already like. In the parable, the Samaritan loved someone who, by society's standards, was his enemy. True love, however, doesn't stop to ask who deserves it. It sees a need and responds with mercy.

One of my favourite examples of this kind of love is the true story of a little girl named Hattie May Wiatt. Years ago, she stood outside a crowded church, turned away because there wasn't enough room in Sunday School. A pastor noticed her, took her hand, and found her a seat. That simple act changed everything. When Hattie later died, her parents found a little red purse containing 57 cents and a note: *"This is to help build the little church bigger so more children can go to Sunday School."* Her gift inspired others, and within five years, that 57 cents multiplied into enough to build what became Grace Baptist Church and Temple University in Philadelphia. One small act of love can ripple for generations.

Loving your neighbour isn't about ability—it's about availability. You may think I'm too shy, or I don't have the right gifts. But Scripture reminds us, *"God has not given us a spirit of fear and timidity, but of power, love, and self-discipline"* (2 Timothy 1:7 NLT). God has equipped you with gifts—hospitality, service, encouragement, compassion—and He calls you to use your gifts for His glory.

Maybe that means baking something for a neighbour, offering to watch their kids, or simply asking, *"How can I pray for you?"* These are small seeds that can grow into eternal fruit.

A little boy once told his coach, *"Let me play today. My dad will be watching from heaven."* He played his heart out, scoring touchdown after touchdown. When asked what changed, he said, *"It's the first time my dad has ever seen me play."* Friend, your Heavenly Father is always watching too—and when you love your neighbour, you bring joy to His heart.

Who in your life right now might God be calling you to *"reach out"* to and show His love in a practical way? Ask God today to open your eyes to someone who needs love, compassion, or hope. Then take that first step of faith and *"go and do the same."*

> *"Heavenly Father, thank You for showing me what true love looks like through Jesus. Help me to see others the way You see them. Give me the courage to reach out, the compassion to care, and the faith to act. Teach me to love my neighbour not just in words, but in action. In the name of Jesus, my Lord and Saviour, I ask these things, Amen."*

FINDING COURAGE IN CHRIST

Read: Exodus 3:4-4:17

On September 3, 1939, as war loomed over Europe, Winston Churchill's steady voice echoed across the British Commonwealth. "We shall defend our island whatever the cost may be," he declared. "We shall fight on the beaches… we shall never surrender." His words called a nation to courage—to stand firm in the face of fear and uncertainty.

That same call to courage today resonates through Scripture. Just as Churchill called upon, encouraged, and equipped his people, God does the same for His children. In Exodus 3 and 4, we see this beautifully illustrated through the story of Moses. God called Moses, encouraged him in his doubts, and equipped him for the task ahead. Through Christ, He still does the same for us today. Let's look at how God calls us, encourages us, and equips us.

When God called to Moses from the burning bush, everything changed. "*When the Lord saw Moses coming to take a closer look, God called to him from the middle of the bush, 'Moses! Moses!' 'Here I am!' Moses replied"* (Exodus 3:4 NLT). God's call was clear, yet Moses hesitated. He doubted his ability and even protested the mission God had given him.

Many people today still hesitate when God calls. Some feel unworthy or unequipped, while others resist altogether. But God's call is always purposeful. He first calls us to Himself—to know Him through faith in His Son, Jesus Christ—and then He calls us to serve Him.

When Moses doubted his ability, God encouraged him with a powerful promise: *"I will be with you"* (Exodus 3:12 NLT). That assurance gave Moses courage to face Pharaoh.

God offers that same encouragement to every believer. (Philippians 4:13 NLT) reminds us, *"For I can do everything through Christ, who gives me strength."* And Jesus told His followers, *"Here on earth you will have many trials and sorrows. But take heart, because I have overcome the world"* (John 16:33 NLT).

Courage is not found in self-confidence but in Christ-confidence. The presence of Jesus in our lives gives us the strength to move forward even when fear and uncertainty surround us.

When Moses continued to question his abilities, God equipped him with everything he needed—signs, words, and even the help of his brother Aaron (Exodus 4:1–17). God provided every resource for the task ahead.

An old familiar saying is that God does not call the equipped; He equips those He calls. Whatever God asks of us, He will provide the strength, wisdom, and courage to fulfill it. (Psalm 46:1 NLT) declares, *"God is our refuge and strength, always ready to help in times of trouble."*

Before anyone can serve God faithfully, they must first know Him personally. Many believe that being *"good"* is enough to reach heaven, but Scripture says otherwise. *"We are all infected and impure with sin. When we display our righteous deeds, they are nothing but filthy rags"* (Isaiah 64:6 NLT).

The good news is that God offers salvation freely through His Son. *"For this is how God loved the world: He gave his one and only Son, so that everyone who believes in him will not perish but have eternal life"* (John 3:16 NLT).

The Apostle Paul in (Romans 10:9 NLT) tells us that, *"If you openly declare that Jesus is Lord and believe in your heart that God raised him from the dead, you will be saved."*

Jesus Himself said, "*For the Son of Man came to seek and save those who are lost*" (Luke 19:10 NLT). The greatest act of courage a person can take is to surrender their life to Jesus Christ—to turn from sin and trust Him fully. In that moment, fear is replaced by faith, and death is replaced by eternal life.

For those who already know Jesus, courage means living out the Great Commission. "*Therefore, go and make disciples of all the nations, baptizing them in the name of the Father and the Son and the Holy Spirit. Teach these new disciples to obey all the commands I have given you. And be sure of this: I am with you always, even to the end of the age*" (Matthew 28:19–20 NLT).

Courage in Christ looks like compassion in action, truth spoken in love, and faith lived out in a world that often resists it. As (1 Corinthians 16:13 NLT) reminds us, "*Be on guard. Stand firm in the faith. Be courageous. Be strong.*"

Every believer can rest in this promise: when God calls, He also encourages and equips. So, let's stand on the promise that through Christ, His strength becomes our courage.

> *"Thank You, Lord, for calling, encouraging, and equipping Your people. Help me to listen when You speak and to follow where You lead. Give me the courage to face the challenges of life, the strength to serve faithfully, and the faith to trust You completely. In Jesus name I pray, Amen."*

A Future With Hope

Read: Jeremiah 29:4-14

Life rarely unfolds the way we would expect it to. Often our plans shift, seasons change, and sometimes the road ahead becomes unfamiliar and unsettling. God's people experienced this feeling well. When we read Jeremiah 29, we find God's people not standing on the brink of the Promised Land but facing seventy years of exile in Babylon because of their disobedience. Yet in that moment—when their future looked uncertain—God sent a message through His prophet Jeremiah, one that is still filled with hope today.

Before we can fully appreciate the promise of Jeremiah 29:11, we must understand the messenger. Jeremiah was often called the weeping prophet, and he lived a life marked by pain, endurance, and faithfulness. For four decades, he proclaimed God's truth to a nation that refused to listen. He was mocked, persecuted, imprisoned, thrown into a pit, dragged to Egypt, and rejected by nearly everyone. By the world's standards, Jeremiah's life looked like a complete failure. He had no wealth, influence, comfort, or applause. Yet in God's eyes, Jeremiah was one of the most successful people in history. Why? Because God measures success not by worldly achievement but by obedience and faithfulness. If you would really like that truth to sink in, I'd encourage you to read these last couple of sentences again.

Moving on, we read that when Jeremiah was speaking to God's people in exile, God tells them to plant gardens, build homes, raise families, seek the welfare of their new city, and remain faithful right where they are. He assures them that although this season is difficult, it is not the end of their story. Then comes the promise we know so well: "*For I know the plans I have for you,*" says the Lord. "*They are plans for good and not for disaster, to give you a future and a hope.*" (Jeremiah 29:11 NLT)

This is a verse many Christians are very familiar with, but it can often be taken out of context. Many read this verse as a guarantee of worldly success—a good job, financial stability, or a comfortable life. But that is not what God was promising. His people were still going to spend seventy years in a foreign land, and many would never return home. The "*plans for good*" did not mean an easy life; it meant that God's purposes were still at work in the midst of hardship. His plans would shape them, refine them, and ultimately restore them.

The reality and truth is that God's idea of success is very different from ours. The world defines success in terms of achievements, wealth, status, or recognition. But Scripture reminds us that none of these things will endure. What's important to God is whether we remain faithful to Him, especially when life gets difficult.

Jesus echoes this truth in John 15 when He says, "*Remain in me… Apart from me you can do nothing.*" Listen closely, true fruit and lasting success flow from a life connected to Him. You see, when we remain in Christ, we will never feel alone. Our efforts have eternal value. Our prayers are heard, and our lives will bear fruit that brings glory to God, not ourselves.

Staying close to God is what made Jeremiah successful. He stood for truth. He resisted false voices, persevered through suffering, and remained faithful to God until the end. He finished his race well—and that's what God desires for every one of us.

Jeremiah's message to exiles long ago still speaks to us today. When life feels unsettled, when plans shift, and when challenges arise, God calls us to remain steady, prayerful, and faithful. He invites us to trust that His purposes are at work even when we cannot see them. And He gives us this promise: "*In those days when you pray, I will listen. If you look for me wholeheartedly, you will find me. I will be found by you.*" (*Jeremiah 29:12-14 NLT*)

So, as this devotion draws to an end, remember that whatever season you find yourself in, whether it be transition, uncertainty, waiting, or difficulty—seek the Lord with your whole heart and remain in Him. Trust that His plans for you are good, even if they don't look like the world's version of success. Because in God's eyes, faithfulness is success. And for those who seek Him, He will always be found.

"Heavenly Father, today I thank You for being a God who sees me, hears me, and walks with me in every season of my life. When the road ahead becomes uncertain, help me remain rooted in You. Teach me to value obedience over achievement and faithfulness over worldly success. Strengthen me to endure, like Jeremiah, and to trust Your good plans even when I cannot see the outcome, Amen."

THE SECRET TO SERVANTHOOD

Read: Luke 17:7-10

We don't have to look far to recognize that we are living in a "me first" culture. Everywhere we turn, we're told to prioritize ourselves—our self-image, our self-reliance, our self-actualization. Even children are raised with the constant encouragement to focus on their own dreams and desires. The world is saturated with messages of self, and that mentality even seeps into our churches and spiritual lives. But a "me first" attitude leaves little space for true servanthood, and Jesus calls us to something much deeper.

In (Luke 17:7–10 NLT), Jesus gives His disciples a reality-shifting lesson on what it means to be a servant: *"When a servant comes in from plowing or taking care of sheep, does his master say, 'Come in and eat with me'? No, he says, 'Prepare my meal, put on your apron, and serve me while I eat. Then you can eat later.' And does the master thank the servant for doing what he was told to do? Of course not. In the same way, when you obey me you should say, 'We are unworthy servants who have simply done our duty.'"*

At first glance, this passage feels uncomfortable. But inside it, Jesus reveals some secrets to servanthood. The first secret is…

A Servant's Work Is Not Always Glamorous

Jesus describes a servant coming in from plowing fields or caring for sheep—dirty, sweaty, exhausted. This servant wasn't performing impressive tasks or receiving applause. He was simply doing what needed to be done.

Much of our ministry looks like this. It happens behind the scenes—in kitchens, nurseries, parking lots, classrooms, and prayer closets. It looks like wiping down tables, preparing lessons, comforting children, and cleaning up messes. It's not glamorous, but it is holy. The truth is that real servants of the Lord don't serve for recognition. They serve because their hearts belong to their Master. Secondly…

A Servant's Service Never Ends

In Jesus' teaching, the servant moves straight from outdoor work to serving the master's meal indoors. Servanthood is not a shift we clock in and out of—it is a posture of the heart.

Many Christians serve their family all day, serve their workplace, and then find themselves too exhausted to serve God. But Scripture calls us to *"give ourselves fully to the work of the Lord," remembering that nothing done for Him is ever wasted* (1 Corinthians 15:58 NLT).

Our reward is coming, but it hasn't arrived yet. And until then, we serve with faithfulness. The third secret for today is that…

A Servant Does Not Serve for Praise

Jesus asks, *"Does the master thank the servant?"* His point is not that appreciation is wrong, but that servants do not serve in order to be thanked.

You see, when our hearts serve with expectations, or recognition, affirmation, or acknowledgment, we are setting ourselves up for disappointment. But when we serve God purely out of love and devotion, we will experience freedom. We remember that God owes us nothing, for He has already bought us with the precious blood of Christ (1 Corinthians 6:19–20). Let us never forget that servanthood is not a negotiation—it's a joyful surrender. Now, the final secret taken for our reading today is that…

A Servant Does What Is Expected

Jesus concludes by saying that we should view ourselves as "*un-worthy servants,*" meaning, "*no one owes me anything extra.*" This is the posture of a true servant: humble, willing, and obedient.

When faith becomes about what we can gain, we drift into consumer Christianity. But when our eyes are fixed on the Master, serving becomes an act of worship, not a burden. (Psalm 123:2 NIV) describes it beautifully: "*As the eyes of servants look to the hand of their master… so our eyes look to the Lord our God.*" Servanthood always begins with where we set our gaze.

Wrapping up today's devotion, I'd like to remind you that the secret to servanthood is simply this: A servant serves because they belong to the Master. And the Master has already given them everything. When we surrender daily, guard our spirits from bitterness, and choose servanthood over volunteerism, we reflect Christ Himself—the One who "*came not to be served but to serve.*" There is no higher calling than that.

Now, just before I conclude and you pray, I wanted to leave you with some thought-provoking questions to help you assess your attitude toward servanthood. Ask yourself these questions and meditate on your responses before you pray to the true servant who can teach us all how to serve with the right heart.

Reflection Questions

- Do I see myself more as a volunteer or as a servant? Why?
- Which part of Jesus' teaching in Luke 17:7–10 challenges me the most?
- Is there any ministry where I've been serving with expectations rather than humility?
- What "unglamorous" act of service might God be inviting me into this week?

"*Lord Jesus, thank You for showing me the perfect example of servanthood. Humble my heart and free me from the grip of self-centredness. Teach me to serve not for recognition, but out of love for You. Strengthen my hands for the work You've called me to do, and help me serve with joy, humility, and faithfulness, Amen.*"

WHY DO WE FOLLOW GOD?

When Jesus sat on that hillside and taught what we call the Sermon on the Mount, the crowds were captivated. They weren't drawn by entertainment or miracles that day—they were drawn by truth. Jesus spoke about the things that matter most: heaven, repentance, marriage, purity, prayer, judging, fasting, and how to live a righteous life. And when He finished teaching, Matthew tells us that multitudes of people followed Him (Matt. 8:1).

They didn't just follow Him down the mountain. They followed Him with their lives. They had heard the truth about God, the truth about themselves—and they knew which direction they needed to go.

Even though this happened over two thousand years ago, the same thing still happens today. People of all ages, backgrounds, and cultures continue to follow Jesus. But the question remains: Why? What is it about Jesus Christ that draws people—century after century, life after life—into a relationship with Him? And why do we follow Him today?

Let me share six reasons that will remind us who Jesus is and why our hearts are still drawn to Him.

1. We Follow Him Because of Who He Is

Crowds gather around celebrities because of fame, talent, or power. But the crowds who heard Jesus weren't drawn to a performer—they were drawn to the presence of God.

Jesus didn't pretend to be someone special—He was someone special. The eternal God in human flesh—the promised Messiah. He was the One Israel had waited for. Peter declared it clearly in (Matthew 16:16 NKJV): *"You are the Christ, the Son of the living God."*

We don't follow Jesus because He was simply a wise teacher or a moral example. We follow Him because He is God—the only One worthy of our lives and our worship.

2. We Follow Him Because of What He Did

Just like an athlete earns admiration through achievement, Jesus earned our devotion by His works. He healed the sick. He comforted the grieving. He fed the hungry. He restored the broken. But His greatest work happened on the cross and in the tomb.

On the cross, He took our place. In the tomb, He defeated death and through His resurrection, He became our living Saviour. (Acts 2:21 NKJV) promises, *"Whoever calls upon the name of the Lord shall be saved."* This means we follow Jesus because of the saving work He accomplished once and for all over 2,000 years ago.

3. We Follow Him Because of What He Can Do

Jesus didn't stop working after He rose again—He continues to work today. He forgives sins. He gives new life. He transforms hearts. He brings peace in turmoil. He protects us from the evil around us and the evil within us. 2 Corinthians 5:17 reminds us that in Christ, we become new creations. Old things pass away. Everything becomes new. So, we follow Him because He still changes lives—and we are living proof.

4. We Follow Him Because We Need Him

Just as children need parents and spouses need each other, we all need Jesus. Our greatest needs cannot be met by friends, careers, or even our own strength. (Acts 4:12 NKJV) says, *"Nor is there salvation in any other, for there is no other name under heaven given among men by which we must be saved."* Without Jesus, there is no forgiveness, no hope, no eternal life. This timeless truth tells us that we follow Him because He is the only One who can save.

5. We Follow Him Because He Wants Us

This is one of the most beautiful truths in Scripture: Jesus wants us. God could have chosen angels to proclaim the gospel. He could have written the message of salvation across the sky. But instead, He chose ordinary people like you and me—to know Him and to make Him known. Philippians 1:6 assures us that the good work He started in us, He will complete. Jesus invites us to follow Him because He longs to shape our lives for His glory.

6. We Follow Him Because Others Need Him

We follow Jesus not only for ourselves but for the world around us. Yes, people need food, clothing, justice, and shelter—but their greatest need is a right relationship with God through Christ.

Every person needs salvation. And God has chosen us to carry that message.

Acts of kindness—supporting families, feeding the hungry—are important and necessary. But our deepest calling is to point people to Jesus, because eternity matters. Heaven and hell are real, and every soul needs Christ.

I conclude today with this. The crowds followed Jesus on that mountain long ago because their hearts were stirred by truth. And today, men and women continue to follow Him for the same reasons.

Some have been following Jesus for many years. If this is you, keep going. Press on toward the prize. But if you have been hesitating, uncertain, or waiting for the right moment. Then trust Him now. Scripture says, *"Today is the day of salvation."* Please know that you can begin following Jesus today—because of who He is, what He has done, and what He can do in your life right now.

> *"Lord Jesus, thank You for reminding me why people follow You—because of who You are, what You've done, and what You continue to do in our lives. Stir my heart with a fresh desire to seek You and to trust You more deeply, and help me to share Your love with others who desperately need You. Amen."*

THE GIFT OF PEACE

Read: Luke 2:8-14

Some time ago, in a small town in Ohio, a group of children was going through what must have been one of the most frightening moments of their lives. While they were in school, a tornado warning sounded, and everyone was quickly ushered into the basement. As they huddled together, the storm drew closer, and fear began to spread like wildfire. The principal tried his best to bring calm by starting a song, but the children were too frightened. Tears streamed down their faces.

Then, in the midst of the panic, one teacher with a strong faith leaned over and whispered to a little girl, *"Aren't you forgetting something, Katie? There is a power greater than the storm that will protect us. Just say to yourself, God is with us. Now pass it to the next child."* And so the message went from one trembling child to another: God is with us… God is with us… God is with us.

As these simple words were whispered from ear to ear, something remarkable happened. A sense of calm settled over the group even as the wind still howled outside. The storm still raged, but inside that basement, peace began to replace trembling, and fear slowly melted away.

Let me ask you today: Do you have that kind of peace in your life? If not, would you like to receive the gift of peace that God offers? You can—because true peace does not come from a calm environment, but from a God who dwells within us. (Romans 5:1 NLT) says, "*Since we have been made right in God's sight by faith, we have peace with God because of what Jesus Christ our Lord has done for us.*" That is the foundation of real, lasting peace.

Our scripture reading today takes us back to another moment in history when peace was both promised and needed. On the night Jesus was born, Luke records that angels appeared to shepherds in the fields, proclaiming, "*Glory to God in highest heaven, and peace on earth to those with whom God is pleased*" (Luke 2:14 NLT). Peace had come—but in a far deeper sense than most realized.

History tells us that around this time, Rome was experiencing the Pax Romana, meaning *"The Peace of Rome."* It was a 200-year period with little war and relative stability—at least if you were Roman. For everyone else, it was peace enforced at the tip of a sword. It was peace built on fear, not flourishing. In other words, there was peace in the land, but not peace in the heart.

Then, on a quiet night in Bethlehem, heaven broke its silence. The angels announced a peace not based on force or fear but on God's grace. A peace not earned by obedience to Rome but given by the mercy of God. The world had seen many forms of temporary peace. But through Jesus, a new peace was being offered—a peace the world could never create.

Jesus later said in (John 14:27 NLT), "*I am leaving you with a gift—peace of mind and heart. And the peace I give is not like the world gives. So don't be troubled or afraid.*" That tells us something important: the world does offer a kind of peace—but it isn't the real thing.

People today seek peace in all sorts of ways. Some turn to alcohol, others to cigarettes or drugs. Some look for peace in entertainment, relationships, success, or self-medication. There's even a whole culture built around *"finding inner peace"* by repeating calming phrases or staring at candles. But all of this is simply a distraction. It numbs the heart, but it never heals it.

Real peace can only come when we deal with the true source of our turmoil—our sin. (Isaiah 53:5 NIV)says, "*He was pierced for our transgressions… the punishment that brought us peace was upon Him.*"The root of our unrest is spiritual. And the cure is spiritual. Until we face the reality of our sin, we will never find the peace we desperately crave.

The apostle Paul understood this. In (Philippians 4:6–7 NLT), he wrote, "*Don't worry about anything; instead, pray about everything… Then you will experience God's peace, which exceeds anything we can understand.*" Paul's peace wasn't tied to his circumstances. Whether hungry or full, free or imprisoned, he had learned the secret to peace: Christ Himself was his strength (Philippians 4:13).

At the end of Philippians 4, Paul gives us a roadmap for experiencing the peace of God: rejoice always, pray about everything, give thanks continually, and set your mind on what is good, pure, and true. When we do this, Paul says, "*the God of peace will be with you.*"

So let me close with this thought: Peace is not the absence of problems. It is the presence of Christ. The storm may rage around you, but when the Prince of Peace lives within you, you can whisper what those children whispered in the middle of the tornado: "*God is with us.*" And He is—with you, for you, and working in your life even now.

> "*Lord Jesus, thank You for being my Prince of Peace. Help me to turn from the temporary comforts this world offers and lean fully into the lasting peace that comes from You alone. Calm my anxious heart, steady my mind, and teach me to rest in Your presence every day. In Your precious name I pray, Amen.*"

DEMONSTRATING OUR FAITH IN DIFFICULT TIMES

Read: Acts 10

Would you agree that the early Christians lived in difficult times and faced incredible challenges? Absolutely. The book of Acts paints a clear picture of believers who followed Christ at great personal cost. And just as they experienced difficulty then, we, too, live in challenging days. That's why today's devotional is titled "Demonstrating Our Faith in Difficult Times."

In Acts 10, we meet a man who modelled this kind of faith—Cornelius, a Roman centurion living in Caesarea. His story reminds us that faithfulness to Christ has always required courage.

Cornelius lived in a time of violent unrest. Historical records tell us that Caesarea was a place of intense hostility between Romans and Jews. In 66 AD, about twenty thousand Jews were executed in that very city. Rome demanded that Caesar be worshiped as a god, and for a Roman officer to follow Jesus could mean losing everything—status, safety, even life. And yet Scripture describes Cornelius with one powerful word: devout.

"Devout" is an old word, but a rich one. Webster explains it as being deeply committed, serious, and loyal. Cornelius was devoted to God, prayer, and generosity, and he led his entire household spiritually (Acts 10:2). In the face of pressure and danger, he did not hide his beliefs.

And Christians throughout history have done the same. One powerful modern example is Wally Magdangal, a Filipino pastor who led an underground church in Saudi Arabia. Arrested, tortured, and sentenced to die for his faith, he refused to deny Christ. Only hours before his execution, God intervened, and he was released and deported instead. He continued to preach, demonstrating that faith shines brightest in darkness.

But you don't need to be a Roman centurion or a persecuted pastor to display courageous faith. Sometimes faithfulness looks like an elderly woman named Pauline Jacobi, who refused to surrender to fear when a man climbed into her car to rob her. Instead of panicking, she boldly told him about Jesus. Ten minutes later, the man was in tears, asking God for forgiveness. Pauline wasn't hiding her faith—she let it shine.

Jesus calls all of us to that kind of visible, confident faith. Jesus did say that *"You are the light of the world… Don't hide your light under a basket. Let it shine for all to see."* (Matthew 5:14–15 NLT)

We might not face persecution like the early church, but we do face challenges like broken families, rising fear, moral confusion, and a culture increasingly distant from God. The statistics around marriage, faith, and family show a nation moving away from biblical foundations. Yet none of this is a reason to retreat. Instead, it's our moment to stand firm as people of conviction, demonstrating our faith with our words, our choices, and our lives.

Acts 10 also tells us that Cornelius led his entire household in the fear of the Lord. Joshua declared, *"As for me and my house, we will serve the Lord."* (Joshua 24:15 NIV) If families today are going to thrive spiritually, they need that same kind of faith and leadership lived out in the home. Studies continue to show that when both parents actively follow Christ, nearly three-quarters of their children continue in the faith. Faith that is demonstrated is faith that is passed on.

Cornelius lived in difficult times—so do we. But the good news is that God has not changed. His Word has not changed. His purpose for us has not changed. And His call for His people to boldly demonstrate their faith has not changed.

So today, may we ask the Lord to prepare us—to strengthen us—to live as His light in these days. May He make us *"a sanctuary,"* devoted to Him in every part of our lives. And may others see in us what the world saw in Cornelius: a faith that stands firm, speaks boldly, gives generously, and points others to Jesus.

> *"Lord, thank You for calling us to live out our faith even in difficult times. Give us courage, devotion, and a heart that shines Your light wherever we go. Strengthen us through Your Spirit to stand firm and honour You in all we do. In Jesus' name and for His glory, Amen."*

THINGS THAT CAN BRING REVIVAL

Read: 1 Samuel 7:1-9

When we hear the word revival, many of us imagine packed churches, overflowing baptisteries, or communities transformed by the power of God. But have you ever paused and imagined what a true spiritual revival would look like right where you live? Picture your neighbourhood, your city, your community stirred by the Spirit of God—hearts softened, lives changed, families restored, and people coming to Jesus in remarkable numbers. In a world marked by fear, confusion, cultural division, and global instability, revival is not just desirable—it's essential. The good news is that the assurance and hope our generation needs cannot be promised by any government, but they are promised by God.

In 1 Samuel 7:1–9, we find a moment in Israel's history where a revival breaks out. After years of spiritual drifting, God's people finally reach a turning point. Scripture says, "*the ark remained in Kiriath-jearim for a long time—twenty years in all. During that time all Israel mourned because it seemed the LORD had abandoned them" (v. 2, NLT).* The word mourned—or lamented—is a key to understanding revival's beginning. Let's look at some ways our faith could hopefully encourage a revival in our lifetime.

The first thing we can do is…

1. Lament—A Deep Cry of the Heart

God's people didn't simply feel sad; the Hebrew idea of lament describes groaning, wailing, and crying out from the depths of the soul. Revival begins when God's people collectively feel the weight of spiritual need and long for His presence again. Verse 2 emphasizes that *"the entire house of Israel"* lamented. It wasn't one or two individuals—it was the whole community united in their desire for God to move.

This unified cry is the spark of revival. When a church, a community, or even a nation begins to hunger again for God's presence, it creates an atmosphere where God delights to work. Revival begins with the recognition that we need Him more than anything else.

Now, the second thing we can do is…

2. Return to the Lord with Your Whole Heart

Samuel responds to the people's lament by calling them to action: *"If you are really serious about wanting to return to the LORD, get rid of your foreign gods and your images of Ashtoreth. Determine to obey only the LORD; then he will rescue you from the Philistines"* (1 Samuel 7:3, NLT).

Revival requires inward honesty. Many people profess faith, but not everyone follows the Lord wholeheartedly. Returning to God involves examining ourselves—our devotional life, prayer habits, service, desires, and priorities. David understood this when he told Solomon, *"Worship and serve him with your whole heart and a willing mind"* (1 Chronicles 28:9, NLT). And again in (Psalm 103:1 NLT), *"Let all that I am praise the LORD; with my whole heart, I will praise his holy name."*

A whole-hearted return involves giving God our best—not our leftovers, not our spare time, not what remains after we pursue every other desire. Like the football player in Facing the Giants who only discovered his full potential when he gave everything he had, revival may break out when God's people give Him their all. When believers serve, worship, and obey Him wholeheartedly, the world around them cannot help but take notice.

Another thing we can do is…

3. Put Away Foreign Gods and Remove the Rivals

Samuel continues, *"Get rid of your foreign gods… and serve him only"* (1 Samuel 7:3, NLT). Ancient Israel worshiped Baal, Ashtoreth, and the gods of surrounding nations. Our modern idols may not be carved statues, but they are just as real: money, success, comfort, schedules, self-reliance, entertainment, sports, career, and countless other pursuits that quietly replace God as our top priority.

Revival requires a surrender of control. It requires identifying the *"foreign gods"* of our lives and laying them down. Revival cannot flourish where idols rule, because idols demand pieces of our heart that belong to God alone. When we put away these rivals and allow God to take over, we position ourselves for His transforming work.

So, what could happen if we attempt these things in faith? Well, what happened when Israel obeyed? *"So they gathered at Mizpah and… confessed, 'We have sinned against the LORD'"* (v. 6, NLT). You see, when God's people united in repentance, confession, worship, and surrender, revival began. Their enemies noticed, the spiritual atmosphere shifted, and God demonstrated His power on their behalf.

Revival is not a mysterious event reserved for the history books. It's the natural result of a people who lament, return, and remove the rivals to God's rule. These elements are as relevant today as they were in Samuel's day. What God did then, He can do now—right here, in our community, in our church, in our homes.

May we be a people who cry out to God, return wholeheartedly, and put away every competing love. If we do, we may one day look back and tell people that we experienced a revival.

> *"Heavenly Father, I come before You with a humble heart, acknowledging my deep need for Your presence and power. Stir within me a holy longing for revival. Teach me to lament over the things that break Your heart, to return to You with my whole being, and to remove anything that has taken Your rightful place in my life. Lord, pour out Your Spirit, renew my love for You, and let revival begin with me. In the name of Jesus, Amen."*

PIONEERS WANTED

Read: Philippians 1:12-26

If you've ever walked past a store window and seen a help-wanted sign, you know it signals opportunity—there is work to be done. In a spiritual sense, the Church could place a similar sign at its front doors: "Pioneers Wanted. Apply Within." God is always looking for believers who are willing to step into new territory, embrace challenges, and trust Him in unfamiliar places. The kingdom of God advances not by comfort, but by faith and courage. Pioneers are never idle; they are people who allow God to stretch them farther than they expected and use them in ways they never imagined.

The apostle Paul is a great example of a pioneer. His greatest desire was to preach the gospel in Rome—the cultural, political, and economic center of the known world. He wrote, *"I must go on to Rome"* (Acts 19:21, NLT), and later, *"I am eager to come to you in Rome, too, to preach the Good News"* (Romans 1:15, NLT). But God fulfilled Paul's longing in a way Paul never anticipated. Paul wanted to go to Rome as a preacher… but instead he went as a prisoner.

And yet, in God's hands, Paul's imprisonment became a powerful tool for the advancement of the gospel. In Philippians 1:12 (NLT), Paul writes, "*I want you to know, my dear brothers and sisters, that everything that has happened to me here has helped to spread the Good News.*" The word "*spread*" carries the idea of blazing a trail, of pushing into new territory—this is pioneer language. Sometimes God leads His people into new ground through doors they never expected to walk through. But His plans are always better than ours.

Paul shows us three tools that God often uses to shape pioneers for His kingdom.

1. God Uses Our Chains (Philippians 1:12–14)

Paul's chains were not obstacles; they became instruments. As a prisoner under Roman guard, Paul was constantly chained to elite soldiers—four different men every day, rotating every six hours. These soldiers were his mission field. Through Paul's prayers, conversations, and unashamed witness, the gospel spread where it might never have reached otherwise. He later wrote, "*I suffer…even to the point of being chained like a criminal. But the word of God cannot be chained!*" (2 Timothy 2:9, NLT).

Our chains today may not be literal, but they can be just as real: difficult circumstances, limitations, disappointments, or unexpected life changes. The question Paul forces us to wrestle with is this: Will I complain about my situation, or will I rejoice in what God can do through it? A pioneer is someone who sees every chain as a potential bridge for the gospel.

2. God Uses Our Critics (Philippians 1:15–19)

It's hard to imagine someone criticizing Paul—but they did. Some preached Christ sincerely, but others preached with selfish ambition, hoping to make Paul feel worse while he was in chains. Yet Paul responded with freedom and joy: "*But that doesn't matter. Whether their motives are false or genuine, the message about Christ is being preached either way, so I rejoice*" (v. 18, NLT).

Criticism—sometimes even from believers—can discourage those who want to serve God. But pioneers learn what Paul learned: if Christ is being honoured and the gospel is advancing, then no critic can steal their joy. Instead of being distracted by opposition, Paul stayed focused on the mission. True pioneers fix their eyes on the gospel, not on those who misunderstand or oppose them.

3. God Uses Our Crisis (Philippians 1:20–26)

Paul faced a life-or-death situation as he awaited trial in Rome. Yet his prayer was simple: *"I trust that my life will bring honour to Christ, whether I live or die"* (v. 20, NLT). To magnify Christ was his deepest longing. Just as a telescope makes distant stars appear near, the life of a believer in crisis can make Jesus visible and real to those watching.

Paul declared, *"For to me, living means living for Christ, and dying is even better"* (v. 21, NLT). This verse is both a declaration and a test. If someone were to fill in the blanks differently—*"For to me, to live is money…fame…comfort…success"*—then death becomes loss, not gain. But for the pioneer who lives for Christ, every outcome becomes a victory. Whether God sends us into new territory through opportunities or through trials, the purpose remains the same: Christ must be magnified.

God still calls for pioneers today. People who are willing to trust Him in unfamiliar territory. People who are willing to be stretched, challenged, and used. People who say, *"Wherever You lead, Lord—I will follow."*

May we be the kind of believers who step forward when God's sign reads, *"Pioneers Wanted,"* and may we be willing to say with Paul, *"For to me, to live is Christ"*—and then live that way boldly, joyfully, and faithfully.

> *"Heavenly Father, I want to be a pioneer for Your kingdom. Give me courage to step into the new territory You place before me, trusting that You will equip me for every challenge. Help me to see my chains as opportunities, my critics as reminders to stay focused, and my crises as moments to glorify Christ. In Jesus name I ask these things, Amen."*

Sufficient and Sustaining Grace

Read: 2 Corinthians 12:6-10

Missionary J. Hudson Taylor once wrote words that beautifully capture the heart of Christian trust. He said, "It does not matter where He places me or how. That is rather for Him to consider than for me. For the easiest positions, He must give grace; and in the most difficult, His grace is sufficient… In circumstances of great pressure and trial, much strength… His resources are mine, for He is mine!"

Those words lead us to ask two important questions: Is God's grace sufficient? And is God's grace sustaining? Most of us would say yes—but the real test is whether we live out this important truth. If God's grace truly is sufficient and sustaining, it must be evident in our lives, especially during seasons of weakness and hardship.

People don't need to see in order to believe, but those we encounter need to see what we believe. If we say God's grace is enough, then others must see that confidence reflected in how we respond to difficult situations.

The apostle Paul understood this well. In 2 Corinthians 12:6–10 (NLT), Paul speaks openly about a *"thorn in the flesh,"* a painful struggle that humbled him. Three times he begged the Lord to take it away. Each time, God responded with these words, *"My grace is all you need. My power works best in weakness."*

Rather than becoming discouraged, Paul embraced this truth. He concluded, *"For when I am weak, then I am strong."* Paul learned that God's strength is often visible when our own strength is gone.

To better understand grace, it helps to distinguish it from justice and mercy. Justice is getting what we deserve. Mercy is not getting what we deserve, and Grace is receiving what we do not deserve. What we really deserve is eternal separation from God because of sin. Yet, through Jesus Christ, God offers us forgiveness and eternal life.

Scripture speaks of two kinds of grace: saving grace and sustaining grace. Saving grace is how we are brought into a relationship with God. As Ephesians 2:8 (NLT) tells us, *"God saved you by his grace when you believed… it is a gift from God."* This means that salvation is entirely the work of God's grace.

But after salvation, we must also rely on sustaining grace—the grace that carries us through suffering, hardship, and uncertainty.

Few people demonstrate sustaining grace better than the apostle Paul. In 2 Corinthians 11:23–27 (NLT), Paul lists the trials he endured: imprisonments, beatings, lashes, shipwrecks, hunger, sleepless nights, exposure to cold, and betrayal—even from people who claimed to follow Christ.

What stands out is not just what Paul suffered, but his attitude during his suffering. He didn't complain or grumble about his circumstances. Why? Because Paul trusted that God would care for him. He had confidence that God's grace would meet him wherever he was or whatever he was going through.

There is an account in Acts where Paul and Silas were imprisoned, beaten, and chained. Around midnight, instead of despairing, they sang praises to God. That is sustaining grace in action.

God never promised an easy life for anyone. Jesus clearly told us that we would face trouble in this world. But He also promised eternal life and His constant presence. Always remember that in our trials, God does not abandon us—He walks with us.

Paul's thorn in the flesh reminds us that even faithful believers face hardship. Scripture never tells us exactly what that thorn was. It may have been physical, emotional, spiritual, or relational. What matters is that Paul prayed, and God answered—not by removing the thorn, but by providing grace.

Paul reminds us in 1 Corinthians 10:13 (NLT) that, "*God is faithful. He will not allow the temptation to be more than you can stand… he will show you a way out so that you can endure.*"

God knows us completely. He knows our limits, our weaknesses, and our needs. He promises to provide a way forward—not always by removing the trial, but by strengthening us to endure it.

Sometimes God pulls us out of the storm. Other times, He steps into the storm and walks through it with us. Like the familiar words from Footprints in the Sand, when we see only one set of footprints, it is often because God is carrying us.

In the end, Paul learned that God's answer was enough: "*My grace is sufficient for you.*" And that same promise is true for us today. God will give us the grace we need, when we need it, and in the amount we need—because His grace is both sufficient and sustaining.

> *"Heavenly Father, Thank You for Your amazing grace—grace that saves me and grace that will sustain me. When I feel weak, overwhelmed, or uncertain, help me to trust that Your grace is enough. Teach me to depend on You in every season of life. When You do not remove the struggle, give me strength to endure it. Walk with me through every trial, and let my life reflect my confidence in You, Amen."*

Handling Christian Conflict

Read: Galatians 2:11-14

There are very few guarantees in life, and there are some certainties. We all pay taxes, we will all die, and one day we will stand before the Lord to give an account of our lives. And there is another guarantee that many Christians eventually discover: we will experience conflict with other believers at times.

If you have followed Christ for any length of time, chances are you have already encountered Christian conflict—or you will. Scripture does not shy away from this reality. In fact, the Bible gives us a powerful example of how to handle it.

In Galatians 2, the apostle Paul recounts a moment of conflict between two pillars of the early church—Paul himself and the apostle Peter. Just before this confrontation, church leaders had gathered in Jerusalem to settle an important issue: whether Gentile believers needed to obey Jewish laws to be saved. The decision was clear. Salvation is by grace alone, through faith in Christ, for both Jew and Gentile.

Yet sometime later, when Peter visited Antioch, his actions contradicted that truth. Paul writes in Galatians 2:11–14 (NLT) that Peter initially ate with Gentile believers without restriction. But when certain Jewish Christians arrived, Peter withdrew out of fear of criticism. His behaviour sent a dangerous message—that Gentile believers were somehow second-class Christians.

The Apostle Paul could not remain silent. He knew that if this issue was left unaddressed, it would undermine the truth of the gospel.

Sometimes, these types of conflicts are handled in unhealthy ways. Paul could have taken the blind-eye approach, pretending nothing was wrong. But unresolved conflict never disappears; it grows. When issues are ignored, they often fester until they explode, causing even greater damage.

He also could have taken a win-at-all-costs approach, driven by pride rather than love. But Scripture warns us against this. Paul writes in Romans 12:9 (NLT), *"Don't just pretend to love others. Really love them."* And a few verses later, he says, *"Never pay back evil with more evil. Do things in such a way that everyone can see you are honourable"* (Romans 12:17, NLT).

Paul could have chosen a passive-aggressive approach—avoiding Peter while talking about him to others. But gossip never brings healing. It only deepens wounds and damages trust. Instead, Paul models a biblical approach to conflict.

First, Paul attacked the problem, not the person. His concern was not Peter's character, but Peter's conduct. Paul explains, *"When I saw that they were not following the truth of the gospel message…"* (Galatians 2:14, NLT). The issue was theological and spiritual, not personal.

Second, Paul dealt with Peter directly. He says plainly, *"I had to oppose him to his face."* Paul did not gossip, slander, or assume motives. He addressed the issue openly and honestly, motivated by love for Peter and his concern for the church.

Third, Paul did not make assumptions. He responded to what he observed, not what he imagined. One of the greatest dangers in the Christian community is allowing incomplete information or secondhand stories to shape our conclusions. Assumptions distort truth, but direct conversation brings clarity.

This confrontation was not destructive—it was necessary. Because

Paul spoke up, the gospel was protected, and unity was preserved. Later in Scripture, we see Paul and Peter continuing faithfully in ministry. Conflict, when handled biblically, can actually strengthen relationships and the church.

Christian conflict does not have to be sinful or divisive. When approached with humility, truth, and love, it can be healthy. The key is to follow Paul's example: confront lovingly, speak truthfully, and always seek the good of Christ's body. I learned once that you can say almost anything to someone, but it's how you say it that makes a difference.

When conflict arises—and it will—may we have the courage to address it biblically, the wisdom to speak graciously, and the humility to listen carefully. In doing so, we will honour Christ and protect the unity of His church.

"Heavenly Father, thank You for Your Word, which teaches me not only what to believe but how to live with one another. When conflict arises in my life, give me wisdom, humility, and love. Help me to address problems honestly without attacking people and guard my heart from pride, gossip, and assumptions. In Jesus name I pray, Amen."

THE LIGHT HAS COME

Read: Luke 2:1-14

The Advent season invites us all to slow down and reflect—not merely on the approach of Christmas, but on the deeper meaning behind it. Advent is a season of waiting, longing, and expectation. It teaches us how to live faithfully between promise and fulfillment, between what God has already done and what He has yet to complete. At its heart, Advent reminds us of this simple and powerful truth: the Light has come.

Luke's Gospel places the birth of Jesus into real history, under the rule of Caesar Augustus, during a census that disrupted ordinary life. God chose not to enter the world quietly in isolation, but right in the middle of political power, human movement, and everyday uncertainty. Into that setting, Jesus was born—humble, vulnerable, and wrapped in cloths. The Light of the world arrived not in a palace, but in a manger.

Luke 2:10–11 (NLT) records the angel's announcement to the

shepherds: "*I bring you good news that will bring great joy to all people. The Saviour—yes, the Messiah, the Lord—has been born today in Bethlehem, the city of David!*"

This is the good news Advent calls us to remember. Jesus did not come only to inspire us, but to save us. His coming brings hope to those who wait, peace to those who are restless, joy to those who are weary, and love to a broken world.

Hope is the confident expectation that God is faithful, even when fulfillment seems delayed. Israel waited centuries for the Messiah, and yet God was never late. The missionary William Carey understood this kind of hope. For years in India, he saw little visible fruit, endured deep personal loss, and watched years of work go up in flames. Still, he trusted the promises of God. Advent teaches us the same—hope is not based on outcomes, but on God's character.

Peace flows from reconciliation with God. The angels declared in Luke 2:14 (NLT), "*Glory to God in highest heaven, and peace on earth to those with whom God is pleased.*" This peace is not the absence of trouble, but the presence of Christ. Horatio Spafford knew that peace. After losing his son, his business in the great Chicago fire, and all four of his daughters in a shipwreck at sea, he could still write, "*It is well with my soul,*" because his peace rested in Christ, not in the circumstances around him.

Joy grows where hope and peace take root. Biblical joy is deeper than happiness; it is anchored in salvation. Adoniram Judson, after decades of suffering and sacrifice in Burma, still spoke of joy because he knew his obedience mattered eternally. Advent joy reminds us that Christ is with us, even when the road is long.

And at the center of it all is **love**. God's love was displayed most unexpectedly—by sending His Son to us. Romans 5:8 (NLT) says, "*God showed his great love for us by sending Christ to die for us while we were still sinners.*" And because God first loved us, we are called to love Him with all our hearts, love our enemies, and love our neighbours as ourselves. This is always a challenging task.

At the center of the Advent wreath stands the Christ candle, reminding us that Jesus fulfills all four previous promises. He is our **Hope**, our **Peace**, our **Joy**, and the greatest expression of **Love**. As John 1:5 (NLT) declares, "*The light shines in the darkness, and the darkness can never extinguish it.*"

When the next Advent season comes along, may we do more than remember the story. May we welcome the Light anew and allow Christ to shine through us—not just at Christmas, but all year long.

"Lord Jesus, thank You for coming into our dark world as the true Light. With this teaching of the Advent season, help me to wait with hope, rest in Your peace, rejoice in Your salvation, and live in Your love. Shape my heart as I reflect on Your coming, and let Your light shine through my words, actions, and relationships throughout the year. In Jesus name I pray, Amen."

DAY 85

The Importance of Attending Church

Read: Hebrews 10:19-25

It doesn't take long after becoming a Christian to notice a difference in church attendance among believers. Some are present whenever the doors are open. Others attend only occasionally, when it fits comfortably into their schedule. This reality raises an important personal question: Where do I fit? More importantly, why does it matter?

The writer of Hebrews helps us answer that question. In Hebrews 10:19–25, we are reminded that because of Jesus' sacrifice, we now have bold access to God. We are invited to draw near with sincere hearts, to hold firmly to the hope we profess, and to encourage one another.

Then comes a clear instruction: *"And let us not neglect our meeting together, as some people do, but encourage one another, especially now that the day of his return is drawing near"* (Hebrews 10:25, NLT).

This passage shows us that gathering with the church is not about checking a religious box; it's about spiritual health and growth. Many of the struggles Christians face—discouragement, spiritual weakness, and wavering faith—are often connected to a sense of distance from the body of Christ. God never designed believers to grow alone.

First, attending church fulfills God's command. Scripture does not present gathering as optional. The word "*neglect*" implies ceasing a regular habit. The early church met frequently, sharing meals, praying together, studying the Word, and encouraging one another. Church was not something they squeezed into their schedules; it shaped the rhythm of their lives. When we gather faithfully, we are simply walking in obedience to God's design.

Our presence also encourages others more than we realize. Simply showing up matters. Like soldiers encouraged when their allies stand beside them in battle, believers are strengthened when they see fellow Christians worshiping, praying, and persevering together. When attendance is strong, encouragement grows. When attendance is weak, discouragement quietly creeps in. God often uses our faithfulness to lift someone else's weary heart.

Second, regular church attendance is essential for spiritual growth. Personal devotions such as these are important, but they were never meant to replace life together in the church. Teaching, worship, prayer, communion, and giving are all part of God's plan to mature His people. Hebrews 5:12–14 reminds us that believers are meant to grow beyond spiritual infancy. When church involvement is inconsistent, spiritual growth often becomes shallow and stagnant.

Worship aligns our hearts with God. Corporate prayer deepens our dependence on Him. Giving will train us in trust and generosity, and sweet fellowship reminds us that faith is lived out in community, not isolation. These truths teach us that a Christian on a steady spiritual diet will grow stronger; however, in contrast, a Christian who regularly skips spiritual nourishment will eventually grow weak.

Third, the church needs its members in order to function properly. Scripture teaches that the church is a body, and every part matters. "*He makes the whole body fit together perfectly. As each part does its own special work, it helps the other parts grow, so that the whole body is healthy and growing and full of love.*" (Ephesians 4:16 NLT)

Attending church as often as we can is not about obligation or tradition; it's about obedience, growth, and love. You see, God calls us to gather together to strengthen our faith, shape and mold our lives by

His Word, and to see His church function as He designed it to. When we commit ourselves to regular fellowship, we not only grow spiritually, but we also encourage others and set an example for those who are young or weak in the faith. Choosing to be present declares that Christ and His church truly matter to us. In a world that constantly pulls us away, faithful church attendance keeps our priorities aligned with God's kingdom. It reminds us that we were never meant to walk this journey of faith alone.

"Thank You for the gift of the church and for placing me within the body of Christ. Forgive me for the times I have treated gathering with Your people as optional rather than essential. Give me a faithful heart that desires to worship, serve, and grow alongside other believers. Teach me to put Your kingdom first in my priorities, my schedule, and my commitments because I want my life to reflect a sincere devotion to You and a deep love for Your people, Amen."

JESUS IS A FRIEND TO THE FALLEN

Read: John 21:1-19

There is a comforting truth woven throughout Scripture: Jesus does not abandon His people when they fall. In John 21, we see the risen Christ revealing Himself not as a distant judge, but as a faithful Friend—especially to those who have failed. Few stories illustrate this more clearly than Jesus' restoration of Peter.

This passage speaks to anyone who has ever felt distant from the Lord, weary in their walk, or burdened by regret. It reminds us that failure is never the end of the story when Jesus is involved. Let's first look at…

1. Peter's Failure

Peter's failure did not begin with his denial—it began earlier, when he started following Jesus *"at a distance."* Despite his bold claims of loyalty, fear overtook him, and he denied even knowing the Lord (see Matthew 26:69–75). When the rooster crowed, and Peter realized what he had done, Scripture tells us he *"wept bitterly."*

Failure always carries pain. Sin robs us of joy, peace, and intimacy with God. Peter felt that loss deeply, and so do we when our hearts drift. The Lord never intended His children to live at arm's length from Him. Yet how easily we slip into distance—neglecting prayer, loosening our devotion to the Word, or allowing spiritual disciplines to fade.

Still, Peter's tears reveal something important: his heart was broken, not hardened. Conviction is evidence that God is still at work. Failure does not disqualify us from grace—it prepares us to receive it. Along with Peter's failure, we also see…

2. Peter's Foolishness

After the resurrection, Peter made a telling decision: "*I'm going fishing*" (John 21:3, NLT). He returned to his old way of life, perhaps convinced his usefulness was over. The others followed him, and together they worked all night—only to catch nothing.

When we step outside God's will, effort does not equal fruitfulness. Jesus later reminds His disciples of this truth: "*Apart from me you can do nothing*" (John 15:5, NLT). Peter's empty nets were not an accident; they were a lesson. Life lived in our own strength may keep us busy, but it rarely brings lasting fulfillment.

Peter's choice also affected others. Drift is rarely private. When one believer grows cold, it often influences those closest to them. Yet even in Peter's foolishness, Jesus had not given up on him.

3. Peter's Friend

At dawn, Jesus stood on the shore. He called out to them, questioned them, and then directed them where to cast their nets. When they obeyed, the nets overflowed. Suddenly, recognition dawned: "*It is the Lord!*" (John 21:7 NLT)

Notice what happens next. Jesus had prepared a fire, bread, and fish. After a long, empty night, the disciples found warmth, provision, and fellowship waiting for them. This is the heart of Jesus toward the fallen—He meets us where we are and provides what we lack.

Then comes the tender restoration. Three times Jesus asks Peter, "*Do you love me?*" (John 21:15–17, NLT) Each question mirrors a denial, but each response opens the door to renewed calling: "*Feed my lambs… Take care of my sheep.*" Jesus does not merely forgive Peter—He restores him and entrusts him with responsibility again. Failure had not changed

Jesus' plan for Peter. Grace had redeemed it.

John 21 assures us that no matter how far we've drifted, Jesus still seeks us out. He calls us to honesty, obedience, and renewed love. The same Saviour who restored Peter stands ready to restore us—not to shame us, but to draw us back into fellowship and fruitful service. This truth means that Jesus truly is a Friend to the fallen.

> *"Lord Jesus, thank You for being patient and faithful even when I fall short. You see my failures, my foolish choices, and the moments when I follow You from a distance—yet You still come looking for me. Forgive me for the times I've relied on my own strength instead of trusting You fully, and I want to thank You for being a Friend who never gives up on me, Amen."*

Read: Exodus 4:10-12

One of the most common struggles believers face is feeling unqualified. We sense God stirring our hearts toward something—service, ministry, obedience, a step of faith—and almost immediately we begin listing reasons why we are not the right person. We feel inadequate, inexperienced, or unsure. Yet Scripture repeatedly reminds us that God does not call people because they are already equipped; He equips those He calls.

This truth is powerfully illustrated in the life of Moses. When God called him to return to Egypt and confront Pharaoh, Moses responded with fear and hesitation. In (Exodus 4:10–12 NLT), Moses pleaded with the Lord, saying, "*O Lord, I'm just not a good speaker. I never have been, and I'm not now, even after you have spoken to me. I'm clumsy with words.*" But the Lord answered him firmly and graciously: "*Who makes a person's mouth? Who decides whether people speak or do not speak, hear or do not hear, see or do not see? Is it not I, the Lord? Now go! I will be with you as you speak, and I will instruct you in what to say."*

God did not deny Moses' weakness—He redefined it. Moses focused on what he lacked, but God pointed to who He is. The ability to speak, to lead, to obey, and to endure does not originate in us; it flows from the One who created us. When God calls us to serve Him, He also promises His presence and His help.

Obedience is the first step in being equipped by God. Obedience reveals spiritual maturity, which is measured not by how long we have been Christians but by how willing we are to respond to God's voice. Mary's response to the angel in (Luke 1:38 NLT) offers a beautiful picture of this kind of obedience. Though young, poor, and seemingly insignificant, she said, *"I am the Lord's servant. May everything you have said about me come true."* Her obedience made room for God to accomplish His purposes through her life.

Unity is another way God equips His people. The Christian life was never meant to be lived alone. Even Moses, who eventually accepted God's call to speak to Pharaoh, never went alone. God sent Aaron to help equip him. (Exodus 4:14) In (Ephesians 4:11–13 NLT), Paul explains that God gives leaders to the church to equip believers for His work, *"Until we come to such unity in our faith and knowledge of God's Son that we will be mature in the Lord."* When believers work together in humility and love, God strengthens His church and advances His mission.

Finally, God equips us through servanthood. Jesus Himself said in (Matthew 20:28 NLT), *"For even the Son of Man came not to be served but to serve others and to give his life as a ransom for many."* True strength in the kingdom of God is found in serving others. When we lay aside our own personal ambition and choose to meet the needs of those around us, God works powerfully through us.

It's easy to believe that God can use *"other people"*—those who are more talented, younger, stronger, or more experienced. But God has always delighted in using ordinary people who are willing to trust Him. Like Isaiah, may our hearts be ready to say, *"Here I am. Send me."* When we respond in obedience, unity, and servanthood, we discover that God truly does equip those He calls.

"Heavenly Father, I thank You for reminding me that my ability is not the measure of Your power. Forgive me for the times I focus on my weaknesses instead of trusting in Your strength. Help me to walk in obedience, to seek unity with other believers, and to serve with humility. When You call, give me the faith to say yes, knowing that You will equip me for every task You place before me. In Christ's name I ask these things, Amen."

DAY 88

Four Verbs To Overcome Trials

Read: James 1:1-12

Trials are unavoidable in the Christians life. The moment we begin to follow Christ, we discover that faith does not remove hardship—it often places us right in the middle of it. The Apostle James understood this well. Writing to believers scattered and suffering, he did not offer shallow comfort or quick fixes. Instead, he gave practical, Spirit-Led instruction on how to overcome trials rather than be overcome by them.

James does this by pointing us to four simple but challenging verbs. They are actually four responses that shape how we walk through our difficult times with faith and maturity. Let's take a closer look at each one.

The first verb James uses feels almost unnatural: "*My brethren, count it all joy when you fall into various trials*" (James 1:2, NKJV). The word count here means to take an account, to deliberately choose how we view something. James is not asking us to enjoy pain or pretend that hardship is easy. He is calling us to see our trials through an eternal lens.

Trials are inevitable, and we will all experience them. They may come unexpectedly, often at inconvenient moments, and in many forms: financial pressure, health concerns, relational strain, or spiritual discouragement. Yet when we count trials as joy, we are choosing not to respond like the world responds—with complaint, bitterness, or despair—but with trust that God is at work.

Let us never forget that our trials identify us with Christ. They remind us that this world is not our final home and that God is shaping something eternal within us. Our joy is not found in the trial itself, but in the God who meets us there.

After we count our trials as joy, James tells us that we should: "... ***know (ing) that the testing of your faith produces patience.***" (James 1:3 NKJV) If our faith is never tested, our faith will never grow. God allows testing not to weaken us, but to strengthen us.

We must know two important truths. First, our faith will be tested. This is not a sign of God's absence, but often evidence of His involvement. Second, these tests work for us, not against us. Like gold refined in fire, genuine faith is proven through pressure.

Patience and perseverance do not develop in comfort. They will grow when we remain faithful in times of difficulty. God will use trials to deepen our trust, refine our character, and prepare us for what lies ahead.

James continues, "*But **let** patience have its perfect work, that you may be perfect and complete, lacking nothing.*" (James 1:4, NKJV) This verb—let—means to freely allow. God does not force spiritual growth upon us. He invites our cooperation.

It is possible to resist what God wants to do in a trial, or to surrender to His shaping hand. Maturity comes when we allow patience to complete its work, trusting that God knows what He is doing even when we don't.

God's goal is not that we simply survive trials, but that we are transformed through them. Just as children are meant to grow into maturity, God's desire for His children is to grow strong, steady, and spiritually complete.

Finally, with our last verb, James offers encouragement filled with grace: "*If any of you lacks wisdom, let him **ask** of God, who gives to all liberally and without reproach, and it will be given to him.*" (James 1:5, NKJV) When trials confuse us, wisdom is what we need most.

Wisdom helps us understand how to respond, endure, and glorify

God in the midst of our difficulties. God promises in His word to give this wisdom generously when we ask in faith.

Today's passage ends with a promise: *"Blessed is the man who endures temptation; for when he has been approved, he will receive the crown of life which the Lord has promised to those who love Him."* (James 1:12, NKJV) According to this verse, our outlook truly does determine our outcome. When we **count, know, let,** and **ask,** we will discover that our trials will become instruments of grace that will draw us closer to Christ and prepare us for an eternal reward.

> *"Heavenly Father, you know the trials I am facing today—the ones that weigh on my heart and test my faith. Help me to count them as joy, knowing You are at work. Give me understanding when I struggle to see Your purpose, and patience as You build perseverance in me. In the matchless name of Jesus, Amen."*

GET INTO THE GAME

Read: Acts 6:1-7

It's easy to admire a great team from the sidelines. History remembers the 1972 Miami Dolphins as the only NFL team to go undefeated. Yet, most people couldn't name a single defensive player. They were known as the "No-Name Defence." What made them great wasn't individual fame but total commitment. Every player executed his role with excellence, holding nothing back for the sake of the team.

That picture speaks powerfully to our faith. God never intended His people to be spectators. When we come to know Christ, He calls us to get into the game—to actively participate in His work with our whole hearts.

The early church faced this very challenge. In Acts 6:1–7 (NLT), the number of believers was rapidly multiplying, and a practical problem emerged. Some widows were being overlooked in the daily distribution of food. Rather than ignoring the issue or trying to do everything themselves, the apostles invited others to step into the work. Seven men were chosen, prayed over, and entrusted with responsibility.

What happened next was remarkable. Once more, people got into the game, "*God's message continued to spread. The number of believers greatly increased*" (Acts 6:7 NLT). Growth followed participation. The church flourished because everyone did something.

That truth still holds true today. God has a position for every believer on His team. Yet many Christians quietly believe a damaging lie: "*I don't really have anything to offer.*" Others think their role is too small to matter. "*I just hand out bulletins.*" "*I just serve coffee.*" "*I just pray.*" But Scripture speaks clearly: "*Nothing you do for the Lord is ever useless*" (1 Corinthians 15:58 NLT).

No act done for Christ is insignificant. What may feel small to you can have an eternal impact. Sometimes the most powerful ministry happens quietly, behind the scenes, or in unseen moments of faithfulness. Encouragement written in a card, a prayer whispered for someone by name, a faithful presence week after week—these are not "*lesser*" roles. They are essential ones.

Once we accept that we have a place on God's team, the next step is discovering where we fit. Finding your position doesn't always begin with passion. Often, it begins with availability. Many believers step into a role simply because there is a need, and over time, God shapes their hearts and reveals a deeper calling. What matters most is willingness— saying yes and trusting God to direct your steps.

And when God shows you where to serve, He invites you to stay faithful there. Paul urges believers to be "*steadfast, immovable, always abounding in the work of the Lord*" (1 Corinthians 15:58, NKJV). Serving Christ wholeheartedly is not always easy. There are long days, tired nights, and moments when you wonder if it's even worth it.

But Scripture assures us it is never wasted. Jesus reminds His followers that the Father sees what is done in secret and promises reward. When we give our best to Him, we are not foolish—we are faithful. Loving Christ fully may look strange to the world, but heaven calls it wise.

The story of Mary, Martha, and Lazarus beautifully illustrates this truth. Each served Jesus differently—Martha through practical service, Mary through worship, and Lazarus through testimony. Different roles, but equal value, because together they honoured Christ. That is God's design for His church.

So the question for us is simple and personal: Am I in the game? Am I offering God my availability, my gifts, and my faithfulness? As this devotional comes to an end, remember there is still much to do, and God delights in using willing hearts. Remember, you don't need to do everything. But whatever He asks of you, do it with all your heart, soul, and strength.

"Lord, thank You for calling me into Your work, not as a spectator but as a participant in Your kingdom. Forgive me for the times I have held back or believed that my contribution did not matter. Strengthen me to remain faithful when serving You feels difficult or unnoticed. I want to offer You my time, my abilities, and my heart for Your glory, Amen."

LEAVING A GODLY LEGACY

Read: Deuteronomy 11:18-20

Many of us can look back and recognize how influential our parents have been in shaping who we are today. Their love and sacrifices often leave an indelible mark on our hearts. Abraham Lincoln, a man deeply committed to his faith, famously said, "All that I am, or hope to be, I owe to my angel mother." His words remind us of the profound impact a parent's example can have—not just on their children but on the world.

In our final devotion, I'd like to invite you to consider how you can leave a lasting legacy. A legacy that will point others toward God. One that will reflect His love and truth through your actions, words, and life choices. Let's explore how each of us—regardless of our age or life stage—can leave a Godly legacy that will endure beyond our time here on earth.

Let's start with a simple exercise. Think of one word that describes your parents. Maybe it's *"kind," "strong," "faithful,"* or *"selfless."* This exercise isn't just about words; it's about recognizing how our parents have shaped us.

Now, not everyone has had a positive experience with their parents or their upbringing. As sad as that may be, there is still hope for the next generation. The truth is, many parents today face societal pressures that push them into careers, often at the expense of the time they could spend nurturing their families spiritually. But no matter our circumstances, we all have the opportunity—and the responsibility—to leave a Godly legacy.

For parents who still have children under their care, and I'll add grandparents and great grandparents, your calling is to teach your children about God. Scripture makes this clear. In Deuteronomy 11:18-20, Moses instructs parents to *"commit wholeheartedly"* to teaching their children God's laws and His love. He urges them to talk about these truths at home, on the road, before bed, and when they wake up. The Psalmist echoes this in Psalm 78:5-7, emphasizing that each generation must pass on God's commandments so that hope in Him is renewed and preserved.

The importance of this cannot be overstated. If children are not intentionally taught to respect authority, to honour God, and to love His Word, they risk wandering away from the faith. We see it reflected in the rising number of youth leaving the church after high school. But as parents and mentors, if you don't have children, we can change that trajectory by investing in their spiritual development now. Prayerfully, we can ask God to guide us as we teach and exemplify a Spirit-led life.

For parents in their senior years, those whose children have grown and left home, or for those who have never had children, the idea of leaving a legacy takes on new dimensions. Romans 16:13 mentions a mother figure who was like a spiritual mother to the Apostle Paul—*"his dear mother, who has been a mother to me."* This suggests that parenthood isn't limited to biological ties; it can be expressed through mentorship, encouragement, and service to others.

Titus 2:3-5 provides clear guidance: older women are called to teach and mentor the younger women, guiding them in love, purity, and godly living. This biblical concept can also be applied to men and is a powerful reminder that wisdom and experience are gifts God desires us to share. Whether through mentoring young parents or simply offering encouragement, your life can leave a ripple effect of faith and love.

And what about the younger generation? The Bible encourages obedience and respect for parents (Ephesians 6:1-3; Colossians 3:20). These verses remind us that honouring our parents is not just about obeying rules; it's about honouring God Himself. Obedience is a pathway to blessing and longevity, and it's foundational for building a life rooted in faith.

If you are a young person, remember this: you are not just part of the church today, you are also very important to the future of the church. Your choices today—whether in how you respect authority, how you pursue God, or how you serve others—are shaping your legacy. Remember the hymn: *"Trust and obey, for there's no other way to be happy in Jesus."* Your obedience to God and your parents is a declaration that you trust Him to guide your life.

Leaving a Godly legacy isn't reserved for a select few; it's a calling for all of us. It begins with the small, daily acts of faithfulness—praying with your children, mentoring a younger person, respecting your parents, or simply living out your faith transparently. Whether you're young or old, male or female, your life can point others toward Christ.

So today and in the days ahead, I encourage you: consider the legacy you are leaving behind. Ask God for wisdom and strength to live in a way that honours Him and influences others for His kingdom. Your faithfulness today can resonate for generations to come, shaping lives and hearts long after you and I are gone.

In the end, the greatest legacy we can leave is a life that reflects Jesus—one built on love, obedience, and service. This has been my continued personal prayer for many years.

As you reflect on the timeless truths you have experienced within these pages and the journey we've shared over these ninety days, I want to encourage you to read the *Note from the Author* in the following pages. It's written to help you move beyond reflection and into faithful practice—so that what you have learned here can be lived out in your daily life and, by God's grace, become a legacy that will impact generations to come. May God bless you as you continue your journey with Him, guided by the Holy Spirit.

"Lord, I want to leave a legacy for future generations that will honour you and bring you glory. May your Spirit help me to do just that. May those who come after me find me faithful. In your Holy and precious name, Amen."

As you come to the end of *Walking in the Spirit, A 90-Day Journey to a Spirit-led Life*, I want you to know how grateful I am that you have taken this journey. My prayer from the beginning has been that these devotionals would not only draw you closer to Christ but also encourage you to live out what you have learned in everyday faithfulness. God's Word was never meant to stop with us—it is meant to flow through us into the lives of others.

Scripture reminds us, *"Do not merely listen to the word, and so deceive yourselves. Do what it says"* (James 1:22 NIV). One meaningful way we live this out is by helping others grow in their walk with the Lord. If this devotional has been a blessing to you, I invite you to prayerfully consider partnering with me in ministry by sharing it with others. That partnership can take many forms—using this book as a gift for graduates beginning a new chapter of life, for birthdays, anniversaries, Christmas gifts, or special milestones, or recommending it to a friend, small group, or church family who desires to walk more closely with the Holy Spirit.

You may also feel led to help place this devotional into the hands of believers who are hungry for spiritual growth but may not otherwise have access to resources like this. In doing so, you become part of a greater work—sowing seeds of faith and obedience that God can use to bear fruit for generations to come. As Paul reminds us, *"I planted the seed, Apollos watered it, but God has been making it grow"* (1 Corinthians 3:6 NIV). We each have a role to play, and God is faithful to bring the increase in His perfect timing.

If you would like to share how God has used this devotional in your life, or explore ways we can work together to encourage others, I would love to hear from you. You can contact me at **steveranni1966@gmail.com**. Thank you for allowing me to walk alongside you through these pages. May the Lord continue to guide you, strengthen you, and use you to reflect His grace as you walk in the Spirit and live a Spirit-Led life.

Steve Ranni

Reflection & Discussion Questions

While *Walking in the Spirit* is designed to be read personally, spiritual growth often deepens when God's Word is shared within a community. Scripture reminds us that we are called not only to hear the Word, but to live it out together as the body of Christ.

Whether you are reading these devotionals on your own or with a small group, taking time to pause, reflect, and respond can help move truth from the page into your everyday life. These reflections are not meant to be rushed. Allow the Holy Spirit to speak, convict, encourage, and guide as you consider how God's Word applies to your walk with Him.

The following questions are intentionally simple and flexible. They can be used with **any devotional** in this book and are suitable for personal journaling, small groups, leadership teams, or discipleship settings. Use them prayerfully, trusting God to shape your heart and life as you seek to live a Spirit-Led life.

1. **What stood out to you most in today's devotional?**
   Was there a particular Scripture, thought, or phrase that captured your attention or challenged you?

2. **What is the main spiritual theme or truth of this devotional?**
   How does it connect to your current walk with Christ?

3. **How is the Holy Spirit inviting you to respond to what you've read?**
   Is there an attitude to adjust, a habit to form, or a step of obedience to take?

4. **How can you practically apply this truth today or this week?**
   Consider your relationships, work, family life, and personal spiritual disciplines.

5. **What obstacles might make it difficult to live out this devotional?**
   How can prayer, Scripture, or Christian community help you overcome those challenges?

6. **How can this devotional help you encourage or disciple someone else?**
   Is there a person you could pray for, encourage, or walk alongside using this truth?

After reflecting on these questions, take a moment to pray together (or quietly on your own). Ask the Holy Spirit to help you not only understand God's Word, but to live it out faithfully—one step, one day, and one choice at a time.

Acknowledgments

I am very grateful to the biblical institutions that taught me the Word of God and helped prepare me for ministry: New Brunswick Bible Institute in Victoria Corner, New Brunswick; Covington Theological Seminary in Oglethorpe, Georgia; the Canadian Baptists of Atlantic Canada (CBAC), (Lay Pastors Training Program); and the Moody Bible Institute. I am deeply thankful for the solid biblical foundation I received, which God has used in my message preparation over the years and in the writing of these devotions. I also thank all who faithfully give themselves to teaching others the Scriptures.